D0722920

ПА

EDUCATION AND THE UNIVERSITY

EDUCATION &
THE UNIVERSITY

A Sketch for an 'English School'

F. R. LEAVIS

SECOND EDITION

CAMBRIDGE UNIVERSITY PRESS

CAMBRIDGE
LONDON NEW YORK MELBOURNE

Published by the Syndics of the Cambridge University Press
The Pitt Building, Trumpington Street, Cambridge CB2 1RP
Bentley House, 200 Euston Road, London NW1 2DB
32 East 57th Street, New York, NY 10022, USA
296 Beaconsfield Parade, Middle Park, Melbourne 3206, Australia

First published by Chatto and Windus 1943
Second edition 1948
First published by the Cambridge University Press 1979

Printed in the United States of America
First printed in Great Britain by Butler and Tanner Ltd, Frome and
London
Reprinted by the Murray Printing Company, Westford, Mass.

ISBN 0 521 22610 4 hard covers (USA only)
ISBN 0 521 29573 4 paperback

CONTENTS

5

To W.L.C.

' Collaboration, a matter of differences as well as agreements . . .'

PREFACE

CONSIDERATIONS of tact and policy kept me from coming out earlier with something on the lines of what I offer now. But this seems to me a time when, if one thinks one has anything to contribute in regard to the problems to which I address myself, one ought to contribute it for what attention it can get. And at least I am now in a position to say that those problems have formed my main preoccupation for twenty years.

The preoccupation at starting was with the problem of making the study of literature a discipline—not a discipline of scholarly industry and academic method, but a discipline of intelligence and sensibility. Perhaps it sounds less pretentious if I say that I was preoccupied with finding out how to talk to the point about poems, novels and plays, and how to promote intelligent and profitable discussion of them. However, when written exercises—undergraduates' essays and so on—were in question, it was a notion of discipline that had to be invoked. So the concern of the university teacher to make something of his job proved to be not in the least at odds with the aspiring critic's endeavour to make literary criticism something more like a disciplined and relevant use of intelligence than the current books, essays and studies, academic and other, and current reviewing, seemed to represent.

The English School with which I was connected (not always, I ought to say, by very close formal ties) had emancipated literary studies from the linguistic grinds; the candidate for Honours was under no compulsion to spend himself on Anglo-Saxon and the rest. There was, it seemed to me, a corresponding need to insist that such a school must have as its specific discipline, if it was to have any, the discipline of intelligence and sensibility I have spoken of. But, of course, even if one could have been assured of the general acceptance in principle of this idea, principle is one thing and practice another, and they could hardly, in this matter, have been brought into any close relation, except by such a collaborative persistence in experiment and readjustment as one wouldn't light-heartedly count on in the academic world—at any rate in the 'Arts.' Of the futilities, misdirections and wastes commonly incident to academic literary study I have said something in the following pages, and I might very well have said more, with an abundance of illustration. I will merely add here a reference to a danger I have observed to attend upon the kind of literary addiction promoted by an English School that does, to the extent of subordinating the scholarly and the linguistic, lay the stress in a kind of way on the critical approach, though without entertaining any serious idea of discipline. Such a school tends to foster a glib superficiality, a 'literary culture' too like that of those *milieux* in which literary fashions are the social currency—*milieux* of which the frequenters cultivate quickness in the uptake, knowingness about the latest market-quotations, and an impressive range of reference, all at the expense of real intelligence and disinterested understanding, or interest in anything but kudos.

However, the development of my outlook was not occasioned merely by the contemplation of these depressing actualities; it was occasioned as much by direct contemplation of the positive ideal, the discipline, invoked in condemning them. What I mean, as I explain further on, is that the more clearly you see the indispensable value of a real literary training the more is it borne in on you that such a training cannot properly occupy by itself two or three years of a student's university life and that it demands, of its very nature, to be associated with work in

8

other fields. I shall not be understood to be conceding here that the academic tradition of Anglo-Saxon and so on turns out after all to be justified. The conclusion arrived at has a very different force, as I can sufficiently indicate by giving another, though not incompatible, account of the way to it: a serious interest in the possibilities of the study of literature at the university can hardly fail to become a preoccupation with the problem of devising a humane education to take the place of the old, now, in the face of modern conditions, so patently inadequate, and that problem can hardly fail to pose itself as one of bringing into relation a diversity of fields of knowledge and thought.

And when you tackle the problem of humane education you find yourself contemplating the Idea of a University—that Idea which the actuality nowadays tends so little to remind us of, yet with the realization of which in some measure (I argue in the following pages) is bound up what measure of success you can hope for with the educational problem. Further, seeing this, you cannot fail to see that the vindication of the Idea as an operative reality is a matter of the greatest urgency in itself, so that a concern for the Idea of a University in the interests of humane education becomes equally a concern for humane education in the interests of the Idea: a serious tackling of the educational problem recommends itself as a way of bringing Idea and actuality into closer relation.

I enlarge on these points in the chapters that follow, and do this much summarizing here in order to insist on the kind of correlation of concerns that is represented by the linked terms of my main title: I want it to be clear from the outset that I mean 'University' to be as direct and primary a focus as 'Education.' And perhaps I had better insist also on the intention represented by the form of presentation I have adopted. The form, or the part of it

9

I have in mind, is that of a sketch, addressed to specific existing conditions, for a practical experiment at a particular place. The hypothetical nature of the sketch I need hardly insist on: if changes were being contemplated there in view of the urgencies of the time, and if I were a person whose views had weight and whose positive suggestions were invited, these would be the lines of my response.

I adopted this kind of particularity as the best way of enforcing the general application of my theme. There are many varieties of experiment possible on the general lines of my sketch, and it is the general lines that I want to present sharply and convincingly. The only way to do that, so far as I can see, is to present them in terms of a fairly particularized scheme. On the other hand, as I explain in the ensuing chapter, I am anxious to make the practical intention, the directness of the drive at practice, unmistakable, and to avoid any suggestion of the Utopian. Hence, then, the hypothetical start from an actual existing school in a specified university, and hence the hypothetical compromise, with its limiting consequences.

'Practical intention' may evoke ironical pity in some who read this and recall their experience of the academic world. Yet, where the need is so urgent, the faith (if that is the word) involved in carrying on with life makes one put as challengingly as possible the case that looks to one so strong. This is clearly a critical time. It is still possible to say that 'post-war reconstruction' represents opportunities as well as depressing probabilities. An opportunity seized somewhere might, in the shape of impulsion given, standard set, and influence exerted indirectly, have results out of all proportion to the scale of the experiment. And it is easy to imagine the case as one might put it to the academic authority not indisposed to consider for possible sanctioning the kind of experiment in view, or (if imagination may be indulged so far) to the benefactor contemplating the endowment of such an experiment, to be carried on under less limiting conditions, and on a more adequate scale, than I have thought it good tactics to postulate (a reference to Dr. Meiklejohn's 'Experimental College' (see p. 13 below) will explain sufficiently what I mean).

There are, by way of enforcing the essential argument of my first chapter, other emphases that might be laid. Such prepotency as this country may hope for in the English-speaking world of the future must lie in the cultural realm, and that it should exert such a prepotency—as focus of the finer life of cultural tradition (which is a very different matter from being given over to inert traditionalism, academic gentility and museum-conservation of the forms of past life)—is very much to be desired. In the performance of this function the universities have an essential part; a part, in its direct and indirect bearings, so essential that if something is not done—and it must be almost inevitably at an ancient university in the first place—to give new life and body to the Idea of a University, this country will not long retain, and will not deserve to retain, any of the authority and influence belonging to the culturally senior partner (with regard to the possible implications of 'senior' it should be said here that, in these matters, greater maturity means—or should mean—finer and stronger vitality). The university that made a serious and sustained effort, in the spirit suggested, to vindicate the Idea in working out a solution of the key educational problem would not fail of a measure of success sufficient to make a real difference. And it would have a good chance of becoming, if not the Athens of the English-speaking world, the unmistakable main focus of the Athenian function it had done so much to confirm to this country.

In Chapter III of the following I am faced with the rather embarrassing problem of making quite plain what I mean by critical analysis and the training of sensibility. That there should be such a problem seems to me absurd, but there is: in the existing state of criticism and of literary education, even readers who understand quite well the nature of the essential discipline of which I speak may not be sure whether I myself am sound on the point; and, on the other hand, I cannot merely by repudiating the substitutes that have been advertised and exemplified in recent years count on general understanding of what positively I intend. A volume is needed, dealing systematically, in an ordered sequence of demonstrations, with the elements of 'practical criticism,' and showing plainly and at length what analysis is, and what the nature of the essential discipline relevant to literary study. As a footnote to Chapter III intimates, I have committed myself to an offer at filling the gap, and I propose to bring out the book shortly. But it is necessary to the purpose of the present 'sketch' that it should be as far as possible self-contained; and it is peculiarly necessary that what I insist on as the key-discipline shall be a real and effective presence in the reader's consideration of my scheme and argument. So I have given some space in Chapter III to illustration, and have borrowed a page or two from the promised larger volume; to which, I hope, anyone who wants to see the odds and ends of illustration developed in a systematic context will soon be able to refer.

By way of reinforcing my necessarily restricted treatment of the literary part of an education (I had to be careful about the distribution of emphasis in the 'sketch' as a whole), I conclude the present book with an appendix: *How to Teach Reading*. This was written ten years or so ago, when Ezra Pound's *How to Read* gave me, for saying in a concise and challenging way some things that seemed to me to need saying (and in that way), an opportunity I was grateful for. Time has made one or two passages, recommendatory of particular critical aids, obsolete; these I have revised or omitted (making some compensating additions). The touches of 'period' elsewhere there seemed no reason for meddling with: such point and force as the manifesto had remained unaffected. It is some years since the original pamphlet went out of print; and a persistence of inquiries about it has encouraged me in thinking that there is a function for the kind of epitomized statement of principles and elements it essayed.

I have to thank the Editors of *Scrutiny* for permission to use matter that has appeared there.

NOTE: *The Experimental College* by Alexander Meiklejohn was published in 1932 (Harper & Brothers). The experiment it records was authorized by the University of Wisconsin. The Advisers who directed the College were given facilities for working out, in conjunction with a body of students, who (if they satisfied the Advisers) could achieve their degree-qualifications in this way, a modern liberal education. ' " The content of study," the " methods of teaching," the " determining conditions of undergraduate liberal instruction "—all these were to be examined, and the Advisers were set free to do with each of them, with all of them in combination, whatever they might think best.'

Concerning the lines of the experiment enough for the purposes of my argument will come out in the two following chapters. But the book ought to be known.

Chapter I

THE IDEA OF A UNIVERSITY

This closeness of connection between the character of a society and the character of its education cannot be too strongly stressed. Schools and colleges are not something apart from the social order to which they belong. They are that order trying to prepare its youth for participation in its own activities. And a society can only teach the hopes, the knowledge, the values, the beliefs which it has.

ALEXANDER MEIKLEJOHN, *The Experimental College.*

USING the same epigraph on another occasion the present writer opened with this commentary:

If these depressing considerations leave some of us (including Dr. Meiklejohn) still arduously interested in education, it must be because it is still possible to believe that the obvious drift—or drive—of civilization doesn't exhaustively represent 'the hopes, the knowledge, the values, the beliefs' of the society to which we belong. And it is in fact in that society conventionally assumed that education should be in some ways concerned with countering certain characteristic tendencies of civilization. Those of us who are not completely pessimistic are committed to believing that this assumption is in some measure justified by a correspondent reality, one which we ought to do our utmost to make more effective.

In bold moments a complementary proposition to Dr. Meiklejohn's may perhaps be thrown out: namely, that schools and colleges are, or should be, society trying to preserve and develop a continuity of consciousness and a mature directing sense of value—a sense of value informed by a traditional wisdom. Any serious notion of education would seem to invoke both propositions. Their reconciliation in practice, things being as they are to-day, cannot be provided for by any simple formula. A complete and happy reconciliation would clearly involve more than educational reform.

15

EDUCATION AND THE UNIVERSITY

I indicate here the nature both of the problem that must be faced by anyone to-day who proposes to take education seriously, and of the faith in which he must face it. He will inevitably find himself thinking of the problem as one of resisting the bent of civilization in our time—of trying to move against the stream. But if resistance and counter-movement were all there were to it, the effort would not be worth making. Those who find it worth making must feel it to be the insistence of essential human needs; needs manifested in a certain force of tradition that they, in promoting the effort, represent and are endeavouring, by bringing it to greater consciousness of ends and means and urgencies, to strengthen and direct. In despondent moments they may feel that urgency manifests itself to-day in something like a completeness of unconsciousness, and that it is misleading to speak of any relevant tradition as having force. Nevertheless they have to recognize that, actually, cultural tradition relevant to their aims is active and potent in many ways in the life of the community, and notably in education.

I am concerned in these pages with liberal education at the university level (if something effective cannot be done at that level, it would seem vain to hope much of efforts in education at other levels). The universities are recognized symbols of cultural tradition—of cultural tradition still conceived as a directing force, representing a wisdom older than modern civilization and having an authority that should check and control the blind drive onward of material and mechanical development, with its human consequences. The ancient universities are more than symbols; they, at any rate, may fairly be called foci of such a force, capable, by reason of their prestige and their part in the life of the country, of exercising an enormous influence. Much has been compromised there; there, too, unconsciousness gains—it both spreads and deepens;

but they are still in more than form representatives of humane tradition.

'Humane tradition' may seem a vague concept. I don't think that an attempt to define it by an enumeration of its contents would help. It seems to me better to point to English literature, which is unquestionably and producibly 'there,' and to suggest that the 'literary tradition' that this unquestionable existence justifies us in speaking of might also be called a vague concept. And the relation of 'literary tradition' to 'humane tradition' is plainly not the mere external one of a parallel. Here, it may be said in passing, we have a reason for making a scheme of liberal education centre in the study of English literature. But this is a head to be returned to later. The business at the moment is to suggest in what way a serious effort in education must be conceived as the effort of a cultural tradition at maintaining continuity—or in what way such an effort is conceived to be so in these pages.

For I think it worth insisting on the difference, as I see it, between the present approach and the Humanism of Irving Babbitt. It occurred to me to make the dissociation because Mr. T. S. Eliot, referring at the Malvern Conference (in a complimentary way) to an essay of mine the substance of which is included in this book, used the word 'humanist' in commenting on the approach.[1] The accompanying mention of Irving Babbitt made the bracketing force of the word plain. The difference, I might start by saying, is that, whereas Humanism is a doctrine and Irving Babbitt's aim is to state and establish it in general theoretical terms, my own aim is to deal in doctrine, theory and general terms as little as possible. The main concern of these pages is with methods and

---

[1] *Malvern, 1941. Being the Proceedings of the Archbishop of York's Conference.* See Mr. Eliot's address, and, in particular, pages 205 and 208.

tactics; these are what, keeping as close as possible to the practical, they offer. Of course, certain assumptions are implied; these are what I am stating now.

I assume that the attempt to establish a real liberal education in this country—to restore in relation to the modern world the idea of liberal education—is worth making because, in spite of all our talk about disintegration and decay, and in spite of what we feel with so much excuse in our many despondent moments, we still have a positive cultural tradition. Its persistence is such that we can, in attempting at an ancient university an experiment in liberal education, count on a sufficient measure of agreement, overt and implicit, about essential values to make it unnecessary to discuss ultimate sanctions, or provide a philosophy, before starting to work. This I assume; and I believe further that what is unnecessary is best avoided. That is, the kind of effort I have in mind would be the effort of an actual living tradition to bring itself to a focus, and would see itself—or feel itself—in terms of the carrying-on of a going concern. It may be said that here I am offering theory and doctrine; their drift, then, is that we should deal as much as possible in the concrete, the actual and the particular, and not expend ourselves overmuch on the definition or exploration of values and sanctions in the abstract.

Criticizing Babbitt's Humanism Mr. Eliot says:

> It is not at all that Mr. Babbitt has *misunderstood* any of these persons, or that he is not fully acquainted with the civilization out of which they sprang. On the contrary, he knows all about them. It is rather, I think, that in his interest in the messages of individuals—messages conveyed in books—he has tended merely to neglect the conditions. The great men whom he holds up for our admiration and example are torn from their contexts of race, place and time. And in consequence, Mr. Babbitt seems to me to tear himself from his own context.

Here the difference between Humanism and the approach in question in these pages comes out plainly enough. It is a central aim of Babbitt's Humanism that invites this criticism; the aim of arriving with the aid of (among others) Confucius, Buddha, Socrates and Erasmus at definitions of an ideal Humanism or Humanist. But the business of working out in practice at an ancient English university the means of rehabilitating the function of the 'humanities' involves, as I see it, no such undertaking. It is advisedly that I particularize ' ancient English university': the preoccupation is not with the generalities of philosophical and moral theory and doctrine, but with picking up a continuity; carrying on and fostering the essential life of a time-honoured and powerful institution, in this concrete historical England. And the preoccupation of the students in the contemplated school would not be with this and the other selected exemplar—man or book, 'torn from their context of race, place and time.' At the centre of the work, in a way and under conditions to be discussed, would be a study of the literature of their own language and country—the most intimate kind of study, that is, of a concrete tradition. And a study of tradition in literature involves a great deal more than the literary.

Of course, it is the preoccupation with cultural values as human and separable from any particular religious frame or basis, the offer at a cultural regeneration that is not to proceed by way of a religious revival, that prompts the description 'humanist.' Literary criticism must, in this sense, always be humanist; whatever it may end in, it must be humanist in approach, in so far as it is literary criticism and not something else. It seems to me obvious that the approach needed in education must be in the same way humanist. The study of English literature, and not the less so for being controlled by a strict critical discipline, necessarily leads the student, by a variety of approaches, to consider the relation of humane culture to religion, and the place of religion in civilization. The conclusions drawn from such a study may often concur with those expressed by Mr. Eliot in his essay on *The Humanism of Irving Babbitt*. Whether or not this is likely to be so for students who haven't started as adherents of a religious creed there is no immediate need to discuss. The point is that, whatever else may be necessary, there must in any case be, to meet the present crisis of civilization, a liberal education that doesn't start with a doctrinal frame, and is not directed at inculcating one. The Christian comments that the culture represented by such an education is incomplete, and for him, perhaps, the frame will always be there. And when he says that the cultural tradition we belong to and must aim to preserve is in very important senses Christian he commands assent. But this is the age, not of Dante or of Herbert, but of T. S. Eliot; and Eliot's genius, which is of the kind that makes a poet profoundly representative, runs to that marvellous creative originality in the use of language because he cannot, for the ordering of his experience in poetry of directly religious preoccupation, make anything like that direct use of a received doctrinal frame or conceptual apparatus which for Dante or Herbert was natural or inevitable—though the aspiration of Eliot's poetry is given in the declared Anglo-Catholicism and classicism of his prose.

In such an age the business of quickening and concentrating into strong conscious life the cultural sensibility in which tradition has its effective continuance (for the nature of the problem answers to this kind of account) will not be forwarded by any proposal that implies conditions at all analogous to those of the age of Dante. The education that will forward the attainment of a real order cannot offer a comprehensive order either as a scheme mapping out and articulating the fields of study in their inevitable relation to a centre of significance, or as a rewarding realization that is to be the goal. The prevailing spirit must be tentative, and if we are to find an analogy with which to suggest the nature of the key-discipline we must go to *Burnt Norton, Coriolan,* and the other poems of that group rather than to the *Divina Commedia*.[1] Principles, of course, are implied in the measure of tacit agreement—the 'sensibility'—that makes the kind of effort possible, and the discipline would certainly involve exploring them; but to make it a matter of trying to impose in advance the order that can only be expected to emerge in course of time, if things go well with civilization, would be vain.

This, then, is by way of explaining in what sense the present approach is 'humanist,' and of suggesting that, if the kind of education proposed may perhaps be judged 'liberal' in more than one sense of the adjective, nevertheless not all of those who insist on the necessity of a religious approach will feel themselves bound to judge that the endeavour after that kind of educational improvement is no matter for active countenance and co-operation.

The aim is to keep as close as possible to the concrete, and to deal with general considerations in terms related as immediately as possible to practice—or to particular proposals conceived as practical. Prevailing practice and prevailing conditions being what they are, what suggestions—given the measure of actual and tacit agreement about ends that can be counted on for working purposes—might reasonably be made for initiating, at an ancient university, a serious attempt to work out an answer to the

[1] See Appendix I, below. The point is of such radical importance, and the analogy has so close a bearing on the present argument, that I print here my immediately relevant discussion of T. S. Eliot's later poetry—a discussion that appeared as a review when *The Dry Salvages* was published.

educational problem? Any proposals worth advancing at all would involve changes drastic enough to give the advocacy something of a quixotic look to those who know the academic world, but the intention is the reverse of Utopian. So much is it the reverse that the charges of presumption and impertinence will hardly in any case be avoided; but I am convinced that a profitable approach must be by way of practical suggestions directed at particular actual conditions.

Some preliminary canvassing of general considerations is, of course, indispensable. A good tactical opportunity for it was provided, when a start was made some ten years ago in *Scrutiny* towards working out the present approach, by the timely appearance of two American texts: a book, *The Experimental College*, by Alexander Meiklejohn, and an essay, *Thoughts After Flexner*, by Brooks Otis. The book reported an actual experiment in liberal education made at the University of Wisconsin; the essay appeared in a short-lived periodical, *The New Frontier*, run by young graduates of well-known eastern universities.

The setting contemplated by the two authors in their approaches to the common problem is fairly suggested by this, from Dr. Meiklejohn's book:

> Our first aim is not to get liberal thinking done excellently, but to get it done at all. In a word, we must recognize that the drift of American life is against those forms of liberal thinking which seem most essential to its welfare (p. 138).

—a passage that relates interestingly to that quoted as epigraph to this chapter. For 'drift of American life,' of course, we can read 'drift of modern life': American conditions are the conditions of modern civilization, even if the 'drift' has gone further on the other side of the Atlantic than on this. On the one hand there is the enormous technical complexity of civilization, a complexity that could be dealt with only by an answering efficiency of co-ordination—a co-operative concentration of knowledge, understanding and will (and 'understanding' means not merely a grasp of intricacies, but a perceptive wisdom about ends). On the other hand, the social and cultural disintegration that has accompanied the development of the inhumanly complex machinery is destroying what should have controlled the working. It is as if society, in so complicating and extending the machinery of organization, had incurred a progressive debility of consciousness and of the powers of co-ordination and control—had lost intelligence, memory and moral purpose. (Of course—but I had better be explicit—no metaphysic of the collective is implied here; the figurative expressions translate into such terms as my 'tradition, intellectual, moral and humane' and Mr. Brooks Otis's 'capable and influential group of human beings.'[1]) The inadequacy to their function of statesmen and labour-leaders is notorious, depressing and inevitable, and in our time only the very naïve have been able to be exhilarated by the hopes of revolutionaries. The complexities being what they are, the general drift has been technocratic, and the effective conception of the human ends to be served that accompanies a preoccupation with the smooth running of the machinery tends to be a drastically simplified one. The war, by providing imperious immediate ends and immediately all-sufficient motives, has produced a simplification that enables the machinery, now more tyrannically complex than ever before, to run with marvellous efficiency. The greater is the need for insisting on the nature of the problem that the simplification doesn't solve, and on the dangers that, when the war is over, will

---

[1] ' All such " schemes " [of social re-organization] indeed become Utopian and futile in exact proportion to their lack of support by a sufficiently capable and influential group of living human beings. . . .'

be left more menacing than before, though not necessarily more attended to.

It was a romantic and irresponsible vision that, in the Marxising days, acclaimed a human triumph that was to emerge out of catastrophe, and it is a philistine obtuseness that (whatever it may call itself) sees a human triumph in any Utopian consummation of the process of the capitalist era. The problem is to avoid both a breakdown of the machinery and its triumph—a final surrender to it of the human spirit. 'The great social problem of to-day,' says Mr. Otis, 'has thus become entirely a matter of controlling the machine' (the machine on which the 'machinery of civilization' depends). There can be no control without (to revert to the metaphors of 'organism' and 'mind') a higher co-ordination. An urgently necessary work, consequently, is to explore the means of bringing the various essential kinds of specialist knowledge and training into effective relation with informed general intelligence, humane culture, social conscience and political will. Here, in this work, we have the function that is preeminently the university's; if the work is not done there it will not be done anywhere.

The general problem as Mr. Otis states it is to restore 'The unity of the Educated Class, and the unity of the Educated Mind in terms of the ideas of its own age.' Of the intellectuals in the past he says admirably:

> The important point is that they represented the centre of the civilization of their age—not particular and isolated aspects of it, but the whole of it. They had, of course, their varying occupations, their special ignorances—but they were in general aware of their own world at all points. With their common *lingua franca*, their common stock of knowledge, and their common social status, they gradually developed an idea of what the truly 'educated' man should be like, what his rôle in society should be, and in particular what responsibility he had for himself and his world. *This*

class—in short—may be said to have definitely represented and been responsible for civilization in their time.

Any such 'centre'—centre of co-ordination and of consciousness, one may say, pressing Mr. Otis into the context of those metaphors already used—has been virtually lost in the process of disintegration; the process to be discussed in terms of rapid change, mass-production, levelling-down, and, Mr. Otis emphasizes, specialization. Specialization represents the problem in the form in which it confronts one when one is asked how, in practice, the function ascribed to the university is, or can be, performed. It is Mr. Otis's charge that, in American universities, hardly any serious show is made of performing it. ' The task is . . . to devise an education whose method and content will supply to its recipients sufficient common premises and ideas to give them an effective unity and a consequent effective influence on the problems of their own time—to give, in other words, meaning and a common function to the "educated" man . . . *par excellence* the man who is responsible for civilization.' But the academic world is part of the contemporary world, and the university itself has been disabled for the task by the process that makes the task so urgent: the idea of liberal culture has been defeated and dissipated by advancing specialization; and the production of specialists (Mr. Otis can cite so distinguished a reformer as Dr. Flexner) tends to be regarded as the supreme end of the university, its *raison d'être*.

Specialization, of course, is inevitable (though some kinds are not so obviously necessary as others); the problem is to bring the special sciences and studies into significant relation—to discover how to train a kind of central intelligence by or through which they can, somehow, be brought into relation. About the kind of relation into which they can be brought it is not easy to say anything brief and convincing. We cannot lay our plans in the expectation of producing even one modern Leonardo da Vinci, and, on the other hand, a smattering, or even a good deal more, of half a dozen specialisms doesn't make an educated mind. As Mr. Otis says: 'Our great present educational problem is to devise a method of "cultural" instruction which will—in the modern world—take the place of the old "liberal arts."' What he goes on to say enforces the difficulty of the problem:

> This implies—as is indeed self-evident—an enormous effort of synthesis. It is more—infinitely more—than any mere rearrangement of curriculum, which will 'require' so many 'courses' (survey, orientation or what not) illustrating so many facets of the universe, from the standpoint of eminent Specialists in these facets. An education which aims to present the basic *ideas* that express the civilization of our time, must be the result of a genuine philosophical and historical unification, which will exhibit the actual interplay of ideas, influences, and forces, and which will chart in some way their direction and give some glimmer of their meaning. It might not be too much to say that we need for our own age what the *Summa* of Thomas Aquinas was for his.

So stated, the difficulty might well seem paralysing. Our age will, before it can stand in hope of its *Summa*, have been turned into something very different from what it is now. But education cannot wait upon the synthesis, and the 'enormous effort' that makes the synthesis possible will not be merely philosophical; it will be the effort that creates an age, and the educational effort will be an essential part of it. In fact, if we are to restore our chilled courage after Mr. Otis's admirable theoretical statement of the problem we must turn to Dr. Meiklejohn's account of the practical experiment. Where the preoccupation is with immediate practice we find, for 'synthesis,' this:

> The principle here involved is that the greatest need of

26

education just now is coherence, unity of interest and intention. On the one hand, it is imperative that in any group which plans for liberal teaching the different fields of knowledge shall be represented. The diverse elements in the human, the intellectual situation, must all be present. But, on the other hand, the essential task is that of bringing these elements into order, into meaning. And for the accomplishing of that purpose the Advisers are persuaded that the smallness of the planning group is a prime requisite. It must be possible, it must be arranged, that all members of the teaching force shall have genuine and intimate intellectual acquaintance with one another. This is another way of saying that the teachers, as they attempt to educate their pupils, must themselves be gaining education from one another, and from their common enterprise. They must be trying to create the wisdom which they wish to impart.

This passage (it is representative of Dr. Meiklejohn's book) brings home how little the problem can be properly envisaged with an eye fixed narrowly upon the desired student-product of an educational régime—envisaged, that is, in terms merely of a standard 'educated man' to be produced. And the 'common enterprise' described by Dr. Meiklejohn had, we remind ourselves, a university as a background—a background that, ideally, would have been very much more than merely that, for a university should be an inclusive and more complex 'common enterprise.'

In fact, at this point a fresh approach seems indicated. No English reader of Dr. Meiklejohn and Mr. Otis can fail to perceive that the practical problem in this country will be appreciably different from theirs, the 'background' here being so different from that exhibited or implied in their references. It is time to consider what there is to start from here. Perhaps, where the older English universities are concerned, there is something to be set against the general American advantage of greater plasticity. Those who are close to a strong conservative tradition are apt to be more aware of its disadvantages, yet it must be confessed that even Harvard, in the glimpses afforded by Mr. Otis, appears to have suffered a great deal more from the last half-century of civilization than Oxford and Cambridge have done. At any rate, let us take stock of what we are given, to start from, here.

It has, then, to be recognized that a not altogether inconsiderable, if very small, minority do contrive to get something of an education (in the relevant sense of the word) at Oxford and Cambridge, as things are. If the process of their production is considered, it is clearly not to be accounted for in terms of curricula, formal studies and official instruction. Curricula, at the best, give opportunities, and if these are profited by it is mainly owing to the stimulus derived from the general ambience, to the education got in that school of unspecialized intelligence which is created in informal intercourse—intercourse that brings together intellectual appetites from specialisms of all kinds, and from various academic levels. It is, it might be said, because they are so much more than educational institutions that the older universities have this measure of educational virtue.

The effect of these considerations is to suggest a restatement of the problem. We have not to debate whether it is to produce specialists or the 'educated man' that the university should exist. Its essential function involves the production of both—though to say '*the* educated man' is perhaps misleading. The problem is to produce specialists who are in touch with a humane centre, and to produce a centre for them to be in touch with; but this centre is not best conceived as a standard 'educated man.' There will be 'educated men' with various stresses, various tendencies towards specialization. There will be—as there happily are—specialists who will be classifiable equally as 'educated men.' Ortega y Gasset, as quoted by Mr. Otis, speaks of the 'peculiar brutality and aggressive stupidity with which a man comports himself when he knows a great deal about one thing and is totally ignorant of the rest.' Even a specialist who merely knows that there *is* a centre will be better than that. And even the mere specialist to whom this degree of education cannot be ascribed will, in his complacent barbarism, be less completely cut off from the centre if he is in touch with fellow-specialists who are themselves, in some measure, not uneducated.

Seen in this light, the problem of maintaining a 'centre' —a centre that shall favour the utmost possible of communication and co-ordination—does not take on any less importance. And though the functioning of a university, actually and ideally, is so far from being merely a matter of formal provision and official machinery, these can obviously further as well as frustrate: the practical problem is to make such provision as shall innervate the actual functioning, the essential process associated above with informal intercourse. This end would be most effectively sought, it is clear, by experiment in the spirit and manner of the Experimental College. And at this point it is relevant to remind the reader of the education gained by the teachers at Madison from their 'common enterprise,' and to suggest once more that the 'common enterprise,' ideally, would involve a wider active co-operation, and so a larger profit, than it was Dr. Meiklejohn's business to take note of.

In fact, what we find ourselves contemplating is the problem of contriving, in an actual university, to come substantially nearer to realizing the 'Idea of a University.' How to produce the 'educated man'—the man of humane culture who is equipped to be intelligent and

responsible about the problems of contemporary civilization—this is a truly urgent study, but a study that apart
from an adequate preoccupation with the Idea of a
University is likely to end in despair. If the universities
make it possible to hope something of education, that is
because their function, fully performed, comprises so much
more than any talk of education—or of research and
scholarship—can suggest. The full performance of their
inclusive function involves the performance of many functions. By way of indicating the general nature of the
inclusive function as it is conceived here I perhaps may
quote—there is, I think, some point in the quoting—what
I have written elsewhere:

> A university of its very nature (or 'idea'), if it is one at
> all, asserts a contrary view of cultural tradition to the
> Marxian: a view of cultural tradition as representing
> the active function of human intelligence, choice and
> will; that is, as a spiritual force that can direct and
> determine. The promoters of *Scrutiny* didn't say that they
> were bent, in their zeal on behalf of 'the function of criti-
> cism,' on vindicating at the same time 'the Idea of a
> University': they may well have felt that to put it in those
> terms would have been presumptuous and impolitic (they
> were none of them of any academic importance). But in
> planning to do in their own way what clearly couldn't be
> done in the old, they were consciously appealing to the
> idea that it was more than ever the *raison d'être* of a univer-
> sity to be, amid the material pressures and dehumanizing
> complications of the modern world, a focus of humane
> consciousness, a centre where, faced with the specializations
> and distractions in which human ends lose themselves,
> intelligence, bringing to bear a mature sense of values,
> should apply itself to the problems of civilization.

Contemplation of the Idea doesn't conduce to satisfaction with the actual. A relating of specialisms in a non-
specialist centre of consciousness—this is not a process
that, from within an ancient university, one is apt to be

very much aware of. A distinguished war-time migrant remarked to me recently that he found Cambridge, with all its advantages, surprisingly content to be an agglomeration of departments and special studies. In spite of the unsurpassed opportunities for intercourse across the departmental and specialist frontiers, and in spite of its being so much urged in favour of the college system that it favours such intercourse, he found little evidence that the use made of these opportunities amounted to much. It was to this lack of communication, this failure in general intellectual life, that he attributed the neglect in Cambridge of his own field of work, the Social Sciences; and he added that they involved so much bringing together of different special studies that the institution of a school of the Social Sciences would tend very strongly to promote the kind of intercourse the failure of which we were deploring. And it is certainly true that, where the disease and the debility have gone so far, there seems little hope of improvement unless in some kind of formal academic provision designed to bring specialisms into communication. My own postulate, of course, is that, while more than one such move is to be desired, one is pre-eminently necessary—one that should aim at creating a real centre in a school of the humanities: without such a centre, a university, whatever essential functions it performs and whatever improvements are attempted, will remain calamitously remote from the Idea.

The effort, then, to work out the means of educating liberally at the university level must be seen as at the same time an effort to create such a centre or focus within the university. To put it in these terms may seem portentous in the light of the particular proposals that follow. But even the most modest achievement of the kind would be gain, and what seemed insignificant in relation to the complex magnitude of the university might have, directly and indirectly, wide consequences—would have, if the achievement were, on however modest a scale, a real one.

What, then, might be done towards making a School of English a real humane focus in a university, pre-eminently representative of the Idea, and capable of discharging the function of the university in the matter of liberal education?—For seeing the problem in this way, and holding this approach to be the most promising, I have already thrown out some hints of reason, and these, I hope, will have been adequately reinforced by the time the lines of the kind of experiment I should like to see undertaken have been sketched.

Chapter II

A SKETCH FOR AN 'ENGLISH SCHOOL'

CAN any teacher in a university School of English, engaging to-day in the appropriate stocktaking, feel comfortable as he contemplates, in relation to the notions he likes to entertain of his function and responsibility, what is actually, his searching of his experience tells him, effected in their name? Even where literature has been emancipated from linguistic and philology, are things as they should be? Especially here, as a matter of fact, is there uneasiness, following on a confidence that was new twenty years ago. Has English been justifying its recognized position as chief of the humanities and its key responsibility for education? Can it even be said, by standards appropriate to the university level, to have been providing an *education* at all? Mustn't an education, properly so called, involve a discipline? and isn't a discipline notably what English has, in this period of emancipation and high prestige, not provided? The charge is hard to resist, and there is certainly good reason for dissatisfaction.

The more need, then, is there to resist proposals for remedying the defect by bringing in the discipline from outside, whether by reinstating the linguistic and philological compulsions, or introducing some Classics, or having recourse to the new science of Semasiology, or by contriving tests and exercises in 'English Usage' or the 'Use of English.' All these candidates, both the more and the less respectable, are, in relation to an English School, *Ersatz*, and are to be resisted as inimical to the recognition

33

and practice of the essential discipline. The essential discipline of an English School is the literary-critical; it is a true discipline, only in an English School if anywhere will it be fostered, and it is irreplaceable. It trains, in a way no other discipline can, intelligence and sensibility together, cultivating a sensitiveness and precision of response and a delicate integrity of intelligence—intelligence that integrates as well as analyses and must have pertinacity and staying power as well as delicacy.

True, it is a discipline that lends itself to effective recognition in the academic world much less readily than the proposed substitutes do. There might be said to be a natural antipathy between it and the academic mind. And acquaintance with examination papers in 'practical criticism' and with published exercises in up-to-date critical method by advanced academics might be said to justify the most uncomfortable doubts. Yet apart from it literary education is null, and worse. It is what we have to contend and work for. And though we can hardly hope ever to have it in an English School fully as it ought to be, the active informing spirit of the whole, yet formal recognition is something: it permits good work to be done. And a little good work, a little of the real thing, can make a great deal of difference. If he comes on stimulus, demonstration and suggestive practice somewhere, the intelligent man gets his start.

But the difficulties and adverse chances being what they are, we ought to be ready to say very clearly what an English School could, under the right conditions, propose as the scope and profit of a literary training. To talk of training sensibility and intelligence may seem to have a narrowly limiting suggestion, as if it were merely a matter of 'practical criticism' work upon short poems and odds and ends. But of course that kind of work can have continuous developments into the completest kind of interpretative and evaluative criticism. The induction into such advanced work clearly demands a most delicate tact on the part of the guide, and there are considerations to be borne in mind regarding the immaturity and inexperience of undergraduates. But the same considerations apply to work commonly prescribed in academic routine (we wrote essays on Shakespeare at school), and humane education is an accepted institution. What is in question is how the ability to profit by experience, and with it the achievement of maturity, may best be furthered. The kind of work advocated entails, in its irreplaceable discipline, a most independent and responsible exercise of intelligence and judgment on the part of the student. The more advanced the work the more unmistakably is the judgment that is concerned inseparable from that profoundest sense of relative value which determines, or should determine, the important choices of actual life. There is no need to add more at the moment, by way of indicating the inherent educational possibilities of the literary-critical discipline, than that it can, in its peculiar preoccupation with the concrete, provide an incomparably inward and subtle initiation into the nature and significance of tradition.

Nevertheless, no one of even the most fortunate experience can believe that, even if an adequate conception were made fully operative, a literary education would be satisfactory by itself. The more one believes in the relevant discipline, the less is one likely to feel happy about permitting undergraduates to devote the years of an 'Honours' course to literary studies alone. One of the virtues of literary studies is that they lead constantly outside themselves, and, on the other hand, while it is necessary that they should be controlled by a concern for the essential discipline, such a concern, if it is adequate, counts on associated work in other fields. In fact, for those who are seriously interested in it the problem becomes, in an inevitable way that justifies, I think, my conviction that the present approach is a peculiarly appropriate one, the problem we set out to discuss—that of devising an education such as may properly be called liberal.

The daunting nature of the problem came out sufficiently in the introductory view of it. What scheme broad enough to look like a serious bid at a solution will not, in the working, run to dissipation and mere disjointed smattering, set off at the best by a patchy genuineness in one or two special fields? Dr. Meiklejohn's Experimental College, it would seem, can hardly have escaped laying itself open to criticism on these lines. What was admirable about the experiment (and Dr. Meiklejohn's account of it should be known to all who have the problem at heart) was its strenuously experimental nature, and the way it broke free from the consecrated régime of lecture-room and examination-room. But the actual scheme so strenuously put into effect seems to cover with its courage a calamitous disregard for an essential element in any real education: the pursuit of breadth seems calculated to entail a disabling cost. The 'Advisers' were rightly intent on keeping the various particular subjects and interests actively related within an integrating main concern. The nature of the integrating concern may be fairly indicated in a summary way by saying that students were to devote themselves to a comparative study of Athenian civilization and American. We see them, in Dr. Meiklejohn's report of the experiment, tackling this formidable undertaking, by a carefully planned procedure of discussion-classes, seminars and written work, with exhilarating energy; but as we contemplate their movements among the multifarious subjects and interests involved—politics, philosophy, sociology, science, tragedy, the arts and so on—we can't help asking what discipline they are able to stay with long enough for it to be, in any serious sense, a discipline for them. They are required to do a certain amount of work (it clearly can't amount to much) in scientific laboratories, and there is provision for them to watch, and talk with, an artist in his studio. But this kind of thing does nothing towards meeting the essential condition of a real education: that inwardness with a developed discipline which can come only by working and living into it.

Not even to everyone to whom it is as plain as it is to me that Classical Greats don't provide what we are looking for will it be plain that, if the choice lay between the old humane education, so represented, and what the Experimental College offers, we should do well to abandon the old for the new. But of course the choice is not limited in this way. So that I can, without at once throwing up the problem, observe that the kinds of discipline and training pre-eminently represented by Greats don't seem to me to be really conducive to the ends in view here. In fact, the point is best made by saying that the observation with which I should endeavour to bring home the deficiency of the Experimental College applies as damagingly, I think, to Greats. The observation is provoked when Dr. Meiklejohn's students are asked, without any hint of the real nature of the difficulties that the question covers: 'How much do you think you lost of the Greeks and the Elizabethans by the fact that their writings are inevitably reflections of a way of life different in many respects from ours? How much of your interest and pleasure was derived from the characters and ideas represented? How much from the beauty and power of the ordering and writing? How clearly can you distinguish between the two kinds of satisfaction?' The observation is that if (being English-speaking) you cannot see how impossible it is to read Aeschylus (in English or Greek) as you read Shakespeare, then you cannot really read Shakespeare, and if you cannot read Shakespeare, then your intelligence has missed an essential training—however rigorous the linguistic, logical and philosophical trainings you may have had.

That is, there must be a training of intelligence that is at the same time a training of sensibility; a discipline of thought that is at the same time a discipline in scrupulous sensitiveness of response to delicate organizations of feeling, sensation and imagery. Without that appreciative habituation to the subtleties of language in its most charged and complex uses which the literary-critical discipline is, thinking—thinking to the ends with which humane education should be most concerned—is disabled. And the process of evaluative judgment, implicit or explicit, that is inseparable from the use of intelligence in that discipline is no mere matter of a 'taste' that can be set over against intelligence. When we find Dr. Meiklejohn's men studying *Mourning Becomes Electra* under the head of 'A New House of Atreus' we suspect that, even if they are made, in discussion, to realize something of the feat of abstraction involved in a comparison of a play by Eugene O'Neill with an example of Greek Tragedy, something is still very wrong. And the suspicion is confirmed by the corroborative evidence in Dr. Meiklejohn's book that the Experimental College did not help its students to realize how essential is the rôle of a trained sense of value in the intelligent reading of literature—a shortcoming that, as has been suggested above, reflects on the notion of intelligence, and of its training, operative in the experiment.

The Greats man, of course, will have read his Aeschylus in the Greek and have been formed by real acquaintance with developed disciplines, but I do not think that this superiority entails a superiority in the respect in question. Indeed, I believe that the very superiority carries with it (or tends to carry with it) heavy drawbacks, and that the training, classical and philosophical, tends, in its very efficacy as formative discipline, to result in something from which intelligence has to escape—if it ever sees the need for escaping. The confident 'finish,' the sense of adequacy, the poised and undeveloping quasi-maturity, that commonly results from such a training is what we see represented at an impressive level in Robert Bridges, with his Academy interest in language and technique, and the assurance of judgment that enabled him to apologize, in the name of 'a continuous literary decorum,' [1] for all the manifestations of Hopkins's genius. Bridges' taste, of course, wasn't vulgar, but observation shows that persons of undisturbed classical training ordinarily not only take *A Shropshire Lad* to be poetry of a high order (combining lyric intensity with epigrammatic precision of form), and admire the kind of accomplishment in prose exemplified by (let us discreetly say) C. E. Montague; they seem to be aware of no grounds for not sharing Mr. Belloc's enthusiasm for the genius of Dr. P. G. Wodehouse. I know of no evidence that a philosophical training tends to better results in this respect.

I shall not, I hope, be supposed to be banishing Classics and Philosophy from my ideal university. I am merely insisting that there is an essential discipline that must be found elsewhere. Unassociated with this, a classical training, whether or not associated with a philosophical, must commonly defeat its avowed and traditional ends—those of liberal education. Nor does a philosophical training in itself tend to produce the kind of intelligence we should be aiming at. And it is not in philosophy that we can hope to find that necessary integration, due provision for which constitutes so formidable a problem.

Of the comprehensive problem, as we have envisaged

[1] *Poems of Gerard Manley Hopkins*, p. 96.

39

it, there will clearly be no one solution. If we are to hope
for anything, it is for various partial and imperfect solutions
at different places, as particular opportunities are seized
and particular conditions taken advantage of. It would
seem to be the most appropriate and persuasive procedure
here to be as concrete as possible, and to suggest how
something might be made of one particular opportunity
that offers at one particular place—the place where the
writer happens to find himself. Particularity of the kind
is essential if the matter is to be carried further, as it seems
urgent it should be; and the given particularity is that
which lies within the scope of the given writer. Statements of general principle may in any case be advanced
without impropriety. Challenged, then, to say how one's
generalities could be brought into any relation with
practice, here is the reply. It is a completion of the statement of principles, of 'general lines,' which without such
elaboration are not really present to be considered. At
the same time the practical intention is completely serious.
If the necessary authority and facilities could be obtained,
some such scheme as this could be made to justify itself
convincingly in practice—the proponent asks nothing
better, the experiment being given a fair chance, than to
be allowed to co-operate in the demonstration: that is
the spirit of the proffered 'sketch.'

And actually the English Tripos at Cambridge, in terms
of which my suggestive illustrations of what seem to me
the most promising lines of experiment are couched,
might be held to be as promising an opportunity as the
academic world has to offer. Firstly, there is the emancipation from Anglo-Saxon and the associated encum-
brances; the school is based, if on anything, on an idea
of criticism as a discipline—of the critical study of literature as a training of sensibility and intelligence. Secondly,
there is the recognition, however inadequate in effect, of

the need both for some work outside the student's own language and for relating literary studies with work that goes outside literature in the restrictive sense. The question is, what might be done to make out of these advantages and formal recognitions something substantial in practice—something as adequate as possible in the way of a 'partial solution.'

The avowed practical spirit in which 'possibility' here has to be understood dictates a considered modesty of proposal—a politic limitation of immediate scope. The aim is to suggest nothing more than, once embodied in the report of an authorized committee, would, it can be imagined, have a good chance of being implemented by authority. That being so, we must recognize at once that there would be no profit in proposing a reform, on the lines in view, of the whole Tripos. For one thing, there would be no chance, under any foreseeable state of university economy, of getting provision for the number of 'lecturers' or 'supervisors' that the inclusive reform would demand. Or perhaps the first criticism that would occur to those whose views would have to be consulted first would be that the imposition of the high standard implied in such proposals would so reduce the number of students reading 'English' as to ruin the finances of the school.

The proposals of the hypothetical scheme, then, concern themselves directly with Part II alone, which is taken by a comparatively small number of students. It can (be it noted by readers unfamiliar with Cambridge arrangements) be proceeded to as their necessary second part by students who have taken parts of other triposes— there is a variety of possible combinations. To attract as many such students as possible would be a part of the aim —as many, that is, of the kind for whom a recognized severity of standard would be one of the attractions. For the reformed Part II—this would be a condition of its influence and importance—would be essentially designed for an élite. That it would, if the design were realized, have an important influence on Part I as well as in other directions, seems reasonable to expect. To be content with modest numbers, but to provide a standard, a centre and a source of stimulus and suggestion—that would be the aim.

For Part II as at present constituted the candidate has to take half a dozen papers (there are certain options) at the end of a course of study of either one or two years. (Most ordinarily the student, having taken his first part at the end of his second year, goes on to qualify for his degree at the end of the third year, but of course it would be in the highest degree desirable that the hypothetical Part II should be normally a two-year affair.) Whether he was proceeding from Part I or not, the Part II student would be assumed to have the equipment that Part I exists to provide. That is, he would be assumed to have a knowledge of English literature from Chaucer to the present day, and (what 'knowledge' here implies) to be practised in judgment, critical analysis and intelligent discussion both of literature and of critical theory—though no formal scheme for Part I is in question, something about the conditions of its efficacy to these ends must be said later. The student coming over from another Tripos would presumably have known beforehand what he was going to do, and have been reading accordingly. With any luck (and such luck oughtn't to be unusual) he would have got his start in the Fifth Form, and provision would have been made at the university to give him during his first two years guidance, stimulus and some help in acquiring critical method. It would be one of the merits of the proposed scheme that it would encourage men to carry on serious reading in English literature while engaged primarily in other studies.

A SKETCH FOR AN 'ENGLISH SCHOOL'

The question, 'Why *English* School?', that might be expected in view of what follows is answered by anticipation. 'English,' because it is a humane school, and the non-specialist intelligence in which the various studies are to find their centre is to be one that gets its own special training in literature. Its special—but not specialist—discipline is to be the literary-critical, a discipline of sensibility, judgment and thought which, of its essential nature, is concerned with training a non-specialist intelligence. About the importance of the special discipline and the seriousness with which it is regarded there must be no doubt. The test by examination would here have a place. Students, whether coming on from Part I or not, would know that, at the end of their course, they would have to take papers of the 'Practical Criticism' kind—there is no reason why there shouldn't be a number of them. On these papers there would be passages of verse and prose to be assigned, on analytic grounds, to period, and also, perhaps, passages to be assigned to their authors. Tests of this kind would be an effective way of insisting on an acquaintance both intelligent and extensive with English Literature. There would also be varied exercises testing perception, judgment and powers of critical analysis. The objections lying against the examination that means a race of the pen against the clock (and a race upon which everything is staked) would not lie against such 'Practical Criticism' papers. There would be no string of essays to scribble in three hours, with journalistic facility and that athletic endurance which has nothing to do with the qualities that should properly be tested; and the clock loses its disturbing power when time is clearly ample for what has to be done. A further requirement would be a number of reviews, some, though not necessarily all, of recent books—reviews of fiction, verse and criticism.

These reviews would not be written under examination-

43

room conditions, and, as has just been intimated, the end-of-course examination would not be the general means of testing and placing. There could be little profit in discussing any mere change in curriculum by itself. Before the board commissioned to adapt the English Tripos in the spirit postulated one would develop criticism and suggestion under three heads : (1) the system of examination; (2) curricula; (3) the system of instruction and guidance. These heads, of course, are closely interdependent, and cannot really be considered apart. But there is good reason for starting with the system of examination. When this is examined, the most enlightened-looking syllabus may turn out to be a delusion; and a normally vicious system of examination will certainly determine the actual 'system of instruction and guidance.' 'Nothing,' says Dr. Meiklejohn, 'is more revealing of the purpose underlying a course of study than the nature of the examination given at its close.'

Judged in this light, the underlying purpose of the English Tripos is to produce journalists. Not that the reading for it doesn't give intelligent men opportunities for educating themselves. But distinction of intelligence, though manifested in a special aptitude for the field of study, will not bring a man a distinguished place in the class-list unless he has also a journalistic facility—a gift of getting promptly off the mark several times in the course of three hours, and a fluency responsive to the clock. Such facility is not the profit towards which a serious critical training—a serious education of any kind—tends, and the intelligent and sensitive, having become more and more aware of the difficulty of thinking anything with precision and delicacy and of writing anything that they can allow to stand, have commonly formed habits that handicap them badly in the examination-room. On the other hand, mere facility, safe from the inhibition that goes with an intelligent interest in the field of study, can and does—the class-lists every year demonstrate it impressively—get Firsts. This facility, of course, is more often than not acquired or improved by hard work; and there we have the most damning way of putting the case against the system: the good student, as things are, is he who studies single-mindedly and undeviatingly how to come out best in the examination (and what doing well in the examination proves is ability to do well in it). The good supervisor is he who 'gets' the best examination-results. Even the supervisor who remains vividly aware that examination-success as an end in itself is not, as a controlling principle of work, congruous with the ends of education finds himself, again and again, answering the innocently practical question with innocently cynical advice—or proffering the advice unasked (he has, after all, a duty to his pupils, and if he is interested in the future of education he reminds himself that a man has no chance of a university post if he doesn't get a First: the system perpetuates itself). Naturally, some supervisors come themselves to assume the principle single-mindedly, and to coach the college team, and exhibit the yearly tale of Firsts, with complete and completely unconscious cynicism.

The fatalism of those (probably the greater number of observers qualified by experience) who would assent substantially to the above account, but who ask, 'What better working system can you suggest?', proves, not how difficult it is to conceive of a better way of testing a student's quality, but how impossible it is to effect radical changes under one of the specified heads without radical changes under the others. For answer the questioner might, if the book had been generally accessible, have been referred to the section on Examinations in *The Experimental College* (pp. 93-96). These pages, of course, lead backwards and onwards into the book at large, for it is no examination-room test that they describe; the grading was determined on the quality of certain 'pieces of work,' representing the sustained constructive effort of a considerable period. 'On the positive side,' says Dr. Meiklejohn, 'the arrangement means that the Advisers will know what, under normal conditions of work, a student is able to do with the sort of task for which education is preparing him. . . . In terms of our working principle we may well ask, Can he study an American community and give an intelligent account of its situation and its experience? Can he read a great book in which one of the best of American minds is discussing our external achievement and our inner life? If a student is able to do these things properly by the use of materials which are available to anyone who normally attempts such a task, then we need not stop to inquire how much he recalls of what he has heard or read.'

It is the spirit of this, and not, of course, any particular formulation, that prompts the reference: the spirit is surely admirable, and the principle invoked sound. The end that should direct and inform the student's work is the acquiring of the relevant and real qualifications— those relevant, that is, to the field of study and to the ends of any serious idea of education: the arrangement that induces him to steer by any other ends—and those represented by the end-of-course examination test are undeniably quite other—is indefensible and disastrous. And though the particular schemes recorded by Dr. Meiklejohn do not, I have said, seem to me to offer anything like a model for imitation, the way he describes of assessing the measure in which the student had qualified himself seems to me to have been, in its general lines, obviously the right.

Our student, then, would be tested mainly by work done during the course, the major part of it substantial pieces of writing of a kind to be described later. As for the 'system of instruction or guidance,' the present provision of lectures and one-hour-a-week 'supervision,' it is widely recognized among both the parties chiefly concerned, doesn't nearly meet the need of the student. What he asks for (and it is the intelligent and self-reliant student whose needs are in question) is not more shepherding, but conditions that would enable him to carry on with independent work more profitably. As things are, left to himself but for lectures, and the one hour's supervision a week, with a vast mass of reading in front of him for dealing with which he has nothing like adequate experience, he is apt to sink into a desperate bored industry—the boredom being the more oppressive because of choked and thwarted interest.

It is absurd that last year's schoolboy should be flung into a wilderness of books and abandoned to his own resources in this way. Officially, of course, lectures are intended to provide the necessary stimulus, guidance, command of instrumental ideas and contact with experienced minds. Officially—but does anyone really suppose they do? Few students suppose it. There was, in the years immediately before the war, a persistent undergraduate voicing of dissatisfaction with lectures, and an accompanying demand—pressed, in fact, to the point of practical initiative—for organized discussion-work. There is no doubt a function for some lectures, but even if lectures were better than they commonly are, the lecture-method could not provide what the student needs.[1] It is plain, on the other hand, that the method of planned and prepared discussion, involving concerted reading and some written work, is capable of most fruitful applications: a full and flexible use of discussion and seminar procedures would be an essential part of the proposed scheme. For the seniors responsible for planning and guidance it would

[1] He certainly doesn't need what he commonly gets. If he wants it he can go to the books it comes from.

mean, of course, labour and exposure to education. But such labour and exposure, once made possible by a properly provided-for system, would be rewards in themselves to those whose satisfaction is in seeing their function justified in effectual practice.

It is now possible, after these preliminaries, to proceed to the major proposal in the matter of curriculum. The English Tripos as it now stands provides, under Part II, for an optional paper called *Special Period of English Literature*, the period varying from year to year. Let us instead (one might say, politicly finding sanction as much as possible in existing provisions) prescribe for all students a study of the Seventeenth Century—the Seventeenth Century, not merely in literature, but as a whole; the Seventeenth Century as a key phase, or passage, in the history of civilization. The seriously and sedulously pursued aim would be to give real effect to the intention represented as things stand by the optional paper on *The English Moralists*, the obligatory paper, *Tragedy*, and the nugatory *Life and Thought* (*Literature, Life and Thought*) provisions of Part I—for the need, recognized in that *Literature, Life and Thought* formula, to relate a literary training to other disciplines and studies gets as things stand little beyond the formal recognition.

The reasons for choosing the given period are contained in that phrase thrown out above, 'key passage in the history of civilization.' The Seventeenth Century is pre-eminently that; and (with, of course, some reference outside) it lends itself admirably to study—integrating study—in terms of England. It is at one end in direct and substantial continuity with the world of Dante, and it shows us at the other a world that has broken irretrievably with the mediaeval order and committed itself completely to the process leading directly and rapidly to what we live in now. In the course of it capitalism 'arrives,' finally

48

overcoming the traditional resistances, so that its ethos becomes accepted as law, morality and controlling spirit in the economic realm; the age of parliamentary rule begins, as does that of economic nationalism; crucial issues in the relations between Church and State, the spiritual and the secular, religion and the individual, are decided in a spirit going against the tradition of centuries —the principle of toleration is established along with that of 'business is business'; the notion of society as an organism gives way to that of society as a joint-stock company [1]; science launches decisively on its triumphant accelerating advance.

The mention of these main heads is enough to enforce the point that the study of the Seventeenth Century is a study of the modern world; that it involves an approach to the characteristic problems of the modern world that answers admirably to our requirements. For the Seventeenth Century is *not* the modern world, and the study of it lends itself to the attainment of those ends which, in the Experimental College as described by Dr. Meiklejohn, were sought through comparative studies of Athenian civilization and modern America. Such a study would have the necessary comprehensiveness, complexity and unity: it would be a study in concrete terms of the relations between the economic, the political, the moral, the spiritual, religion, art and literature, and would involve a critical pondering of standards and key-concepts—order, community, culture, civilization and so on.

It has been assumed that the focus of attention would be in England, but of course there could be no such study of the English Seventeenth Century that didn't go abroad. To say this is to give force to the doubt that must now be anticipated: doesn't the proposed scheme (the full scope of which has not yet been indicated) much exceed the

[1] See R. H. Tawney, *Religion and the Rise of Capitalism*, p. 175.

limits of what can reasonably be considered possible for the student in view? This doubt might be a difficult one to dispose of if the proposal were merely to replace one set of papers by another, equally to be taken at the end of the course as the decisive test by which the candidate is to be placed.—Though it might have been asked in reply whether what is at present formally required of the student is really less formidable—or would be, if the prescription were taken seriously. The answer, of course, as everyone knows, is that prescription is one thing, practice another. The candidate has a great deal of choice, we say, referring to the examination paper. This means in practice that the good student (the kind that gets Firsts) doesn't work at the various prescribed fields to acquire a knowledge that will be tested in the examination-room; he works (inevitably, as things are) *for* the examination, with an economy dictated by a study of back papers (there can't be much variety among fair papers), to acquire a safe minimum, so that he can count on being able to do the duly distributed amount of unloading that can be done in the desperate scribbling of half a dozen three-hour periods. 'These are my three (or four) "questions," with one to spare, in case of bad luck.' That this is the way of working for the Tripos the examiner and the supervisor know as well as the candidate. For the examiner the knowledge is depressing. As he tries to get everything into the paper ('I can't leave so-and-so out: some man may be banking on him') without too obviously repeating last year's questions or producing a draft the size of a pamphlet, a sense of futility is apt to come over him. And (a feeling often expressed) why all this corrugation and sweat over the excogitating of directed question-formulations, when one knows that the candidate will unload anyway what he has ready to deliver on the given topic ('question'), and much in the form in which he has it ready? For the supervisor too the knowledge is depressing, or should be. For the keen and intelligent student it certainly is, as he watches the good student, the 'sure First,' practising Tripos-economy, and realizes how different a thing is disinterested study of a given field from acquiring cannily what can be mobilized to effect in three or four scrawled answers to a three-hour examination paper—a kind of agility that in any case his habits of discipline and conscience (which advanced education should strengthen and refine) inhibit in him.

For the student under the proposed scheme the situation and prospect would be different. He would start under the guidance of an inclusive and unifying purpose. He would have acquired full consciousness of this purpose and its implications (and confidence that it was to be taken seriously and would guide also his advisers and teachers) in preliminary discussions which would have been held at the end of the previous academic year, before the Long Vacation preceding the first formal term of the course. These discussions would have dealt both with the general problem of humane education (*The Experimental College* and any other suitable texts being used) and with the reasons for choosing the Seventeenth Century for special study. Here a second point of difference has been brought in—the use of the methods of discussion and seminar. Discussion-work, co-ordinated with reading and some writing, would be planned to explore key-aspects of the century and cover the main heads of inquiry. And, thirdly, the student would know that, so far as this part of the syllabus was concerned, he would be judged, not on his showing in an end-of-course examination, but on work done during the course, and in particular on three or four careful and extended pieces of writing.

Here some particularity is desirable, and to be able to give the kind of detailed illustration supplied by Dr.

Meiklejohn in his report on the Experimental College would be a great advantage. But this is not a report. And even a detailed tentative scheme for an experimental start presupposes a good deal of collaboration and committee-work, involving consultation with specialists and a play of criticism. However, the possibilities may be sufficiently suggested by jotting down a rough list of heads and topics such as a committee might have before it when organizing work for the year—planning discussions, providing for specialist help and considering what kinds of combination of themes students might be allowed to choose for their extended pieces of writing:

> The background in religious history.
> Calvinism to Puritan individualism.
> Puritan to Nonconformist.
> Church and State.
> Tolerance.
> 'The England of Shakespeare and Bacon was still largely mediaeval.'
> The rise of Capitalism.
> Economic individualism.
> Its alleged relation with Protestantism.
> The causes of the Civil War: the relation between the religious, the political and the economic.
> The reaction against Whig history.
> The Restoration ethos: social, literary and cultural changes.
> The development of Augustanism.
> The new science. Philosophical developments.
> Political thought: 'The great and chief end of men uniting into Commonwealths and putting themselves under government is the preservation of their property.'
> The Revolution of 1688 and its significance.

The social-economic correlations of literary history.

The changing relations between sophisticated and popular culture.

The evidence regarding popular culture.

The significance of the history of the Theatre.

The rise of the Press.

General comparison with French development. Some particular comparisons.

These rough jottings, of course, do not represent anything like an organization of work on the century, and the actual scheme of discussions and seminars could only be determined in immediate touch with practice, and by those empowered and immediately responsible. But the aims would be to provide specialist guidance where necessary, and, while ensuring a due intensiveness of consideration at key-places, to ensure also that, whatever a given student's distribution of interest, he should have an understanding of the main aspects of the century in their mutual relations, a grasp of the lines of co-ordination and the integrating themes, and a due sense both of complexities and of the whole in perspective. As for his 'pieces of work,' the principle controlling his choice of themes (to be determined in consultation with authority) would be that they should entail his approaching the century at different key-points and from different angles, so that, though he wouldn't have distributed his attention equally over the whole century in all its aspects, he would nevertheless have gained a more than superficial acquaintance with the whole. An apparently very limited theme may, in the treatment, become a perspective of a wide and varied range from a particular point of view. For instance, attempting to explain the decisive appearance of modern prose in the first decade of the Restoration, a student would find himself invoking something like the whole history of the century, political, economic, social and intellectual. And the student who, in addition to such a piece of work on prose, should have done one on the relations between sophisticated and popular culture in the period, one on the causes of the Civil War and one on the new science (no pretence of appropriate formulation is made in these suggestions) would have done more than write four essays on circumscribed subjects. He would have acquired a better knowledge of the period than a man, preparing under the present system the sufficient number of likely 'questions' with an eye to what can be unloaded in a half or three-quarter-hour's race against the clock, is likely to acquire of any field of study.

These 'pieces of work' would be done by a student who was participating in relevant discussion-group work (in connection with which there would be a certain amount of writing of the kind a man now does for his supervisor, and, presumably, note-taking), but they would entail sustained independent reading, exploration and following-up. And all this work, of all kinds, would have been done in the light of a dominant preoccupation, a major guiding and sensitizing interest—the preoccupation and the interest represented by another 'piece of work' that the student would have it in front of him to do. This is a summing-up, an evaluating survey, of the changes taking place in the period—the changes as they affect one's sense of England as a civilization, a civilized community, a better or worse place to have been born in, to have belonged to, to have lived in. This requirement would need careful phrasing, but the intention as it is expressed here should be plain enough for the present purpose. The student, it will be seen, would have to ponder his criteria, and that would mean a good deal of thinking and stocktaking of peculiarly valuable kinds. There would obviously be an implicit bearing on the present. In fact, the end would be attained that there was a first thought of seeking through a comparison between Seventeenth-Century England and England of to-day—a comparison the preparation for which might well have started with a reading of Macaulay's third chapter (which should be read in any case).

This evaluating paper brings to the fore the justification for assigning all this non-literary work to an English School. It has already been insisted that the student should be assumed to be qualified in literature—to be critically intelligent about it, to have a trained sensibility and to be familiar with the range, variety and order of the English tradition. This assumption would be backed by the provision, referred to earlier, of papers of a 'Practical Criticism' kind, which every student would be faced with taking at the end of the course and which he would know it was of the utmost importance to make a good showing upon. (There would also be provision for work of this kind during the course.) It is of the essence of the scheme that the work of all kinds would be done by the 'literary mind' (to redeem that label from its injurious use); by, that is, an intelligence with the sensitiveness, the flexibility and the disciplined and mature preoccupation with value that should be the product of a literary training. It is an intelligence so trained that is best fitted to develop into the central kind of mind, the co-ordinating consciousness, capable of performing the function assigned to the class of the educated. And it is in the kind of activity represented specifically by the proposed evaluating 'piece of work' that a literary mind finds its proper development—the completer activity towards which its training tends and which its habit implies.

The extraordinary richness in literature of the Seventeenth Century is one of the reasons for choosing the period. Not of course that it would be merely in a use of the literary evidence that the 'literary mind' would be manifested; it would be present generally in a tact and delicacy of interpretation, an awareness of complexities, and a sense of the subtle ways in which, in a concrete cultural situation, the spiritual and the material are related. But the literature of the century, which bears interesting and illuminating relations to the changing social and cultural background and demands study in that respect, does serve invaluably both as evidence in the ways illustrated by L. C. Knights in *Drama and Society in the Age of Ben Jonson*, and as an index in ways suggested by T. S. Eliot's observation: 'The age of Dryden was still a great age, though beginning to suffer a certain death of the spirit, as the coarsening of its verse-rhythms shows.'

The student capable of appreciating such an observation will not find the summing-up of the century a simple business, yielding an obvious quantity as the result. Just as the most anti-modernist in bias will hardly be able to feel that the changes that produced toleration and the Augustan order were mere loss and decay, so the student most impressed by toleration, the advance of science and industrial skill and the triumph of reasonableness as human achievements will not be able to ignore the loss remarked on by Mr. Eliot and the loss entailed in a new separation between polite and popular culture. For the aim is certainly not that a 'lesson' should be drawn from the Seventeenth Century. The aim is to produce a mind that will approach the problems of modern civilization with an understanding of their origins, a maturity of outlook, and, not a nostalgic addiction to the past, but a sense of human possibilities, difficult of achievement, that traditional cultures bear witness to and that it would be disastrous, in a breach of continuity, to lose sight of for good.

A SKETCH FOR AN 'ENGLISH SCHOOL'

The non-specialist discipline involved in this evaluating of complex and widely comprehensive situations implies, if it is to be a real discipline, and every means must be taken to make it so, some local particularity and precision of knowledge (though not evenly spread over the whole field) and acquaintance with more in the way of particular disciplines than the literary-critical. Thus all students would give some close and sustained study to the causes and issues of the Civil War, whether or not they chose here the theme for one of their special 'pieces of work.' It is difficult to think of a better training than such a study might be in a due sense of the complexities of large political and social issues: no one should be able to carry away from it, and entertain in respect of modern problems, crudely simple notions of the relations between the economic and the moral, the self-interested and the ideal, the material and the spiritual in human affairs. Such a study would mean the acquisition of a good deal of special knowledge in various fields—knowledge, for instance, of the religious and theological background, and of economic and constitutional history. While everyone would read, for example, R. H. Tawney's *Religion and the Rise of Capitalism* (in itself a notable educational experience), those taking one of their major themes from the Civil War would, guided by qualified advice, follow up some of the leads given in the notes at the end of the book. The point is that everyone would have been required to come to fairly close terms—the work must be thorough enough to justify that claim—with other fields of special study, other trained approaches and other disciplines, than the literary.

To offer another illustration: everyone, no doubt, would read Basil Willey's *Seventeenth Century Background*; but any student choosing to do one of his 'pieces of work' on, say, Locke, would (under qualified philosophical

57

guidance) carry his studies a good way outside and beyond that very useful book, which was designed for the literary student. (And a man who had worked on Locke would, of course, have worked on a good deal more than Locke.) Similarly everyone would have used E. A. Burtt's *The Metaphysical Foundations of Modern Science* (if that were recommended by authority as a suitable book), but the student who chose one of his special themes from that field would have had to read a great deal more ambitiously and make acquaintance with representative work on the situation as it is to-day.

Perhaps enough now has been said in this inevitably sketchy way to make plain the lines on which the problem would be tackled—the problem of working out, in relation to modern conditions, a liberal education that, while aiming to promote something better than the calculating minimal acquisition of subsidiary odds and ends, shall avoid promoting industrious dissipation or the mere acquisition of unrelated patches of knowledge. The integrating principle is to be found in the defined scope of the field of study, English civilization in the Seventeenth Century; and its efficacy as an informing principle throughout the course is to be ensured by the student's preoccupation with the final evaluating work that he has before him. The bearing on, the need of reference to and from, the modern world is so essential and inescapable as to answer the purpose that suggested, in the Experimental College, the comparison between Athens and America.

Some critics will still insist that the proposed scheme cannot produce the properly trained man, the man properly trained in anything; that it might be said to aim explicitly at the production of the amateur. The reply must be: Call him what you like; we want to produce a mind that knows what precision and specialist knowledge are, is aware of the kinds not in its own possession that are necessary, has a maturity of outlook such as the study of history ought to produce but even the general historian by profession doesn't always exhibit, and has been trained in a kind of thinking, a scrupulously sensitive yet enterprising use of intelligence, that is of its nature not specialized but cannot be expected without special training—a mind, energetic and resourceful, that will apply itself to the problems of civilization, and eagerly continue to improve its equipment and explore fresh approaches. The education proposed is necessarily full of incompletenesses and imperfections. It is a training in carrying on and going forward in spite of, and in recognition of, incompletenesses and imperfections—the only way in which the required kind of thinking (without which the specialist is frustrate) *can* be carried on. The student is to acquire as a discipline methods and habits that must inevitably be his in subsequent practice if he is to continue using his mind with effect and to the ends desired. The spirit of strict scholarship can be vicious, a mere obstructiveness, a deadness, and an excuse for pusillanimity. Standards, of course, must be maintained. The special discipline of an English School is the literary-critical, and in the field of this discipline such a school would have its function of maintaining standards. With the other studies the case would be different; the responsibility for standards must inevitably lie elsewhere. But that such work at the various extra-literary studies as could be expected in an English School must look oddly unsatisfactory from the relevant departmental points of view is no reason for being afraid to tackle seriously the problem of humane education, and leaving the departments to their largely self-stultifying self-sufficiency.

We should make our dispositions with an eye to producing neither the scholar nor the academic 'star' (the 'high-flyer')—the mind that shines at academic tests and examination gymnastic; but a mind equipped to carry on for itself; trained to work in the conditions in which it will have to work if it is to carry on at all; having sufficient knowledge, experience, self-reliance and staying-power for undertaking, and persisting in, sustained inquiries.

And this is the point at which to bring in a further proposal for a 'piece of work'; and that is, that the student should have to write a paper (a limit of length being given) on the process of change by which the England of the Seventeenth Century turned into the England of to-day. In such a piece of work, clearly, it would be pre-eminently the unacademic virtues [1] that would be demanded and tested: a pioneering spirit; the courage of enormous incompletenesses; the determination to complete the best possible chart with the inevitably patchy and sketchy knowledge that is all one's opportunities permit one to acquire; the judgment and intuition to select drastically yet delicately, and make a little go a long way; the ability to skip and to scamp with wisdom and conscience. There would be some relevant discussions, and the student would be able to consult advisers, and would be told what besides the books of the Hammonds he certainly must know of; but the work would be a test of his power of self-direction.

Since the stress falls for the moment on the prospecting and ranging mind, this seems the place to insert a note on

---

[1] The opposite of the qualities that would be fostered by study in the spirit of the following : ' The study of the classics had, and has, one quite peculiar value, in that it deals with an expression of human experience, which is once for all finished and unchangeable. All rules are definite and all exceptions established in the known literature. The result is that the mind acquires both a precision and a flexibility which the study of no language or science which is still in the course of development can give.'—An ex-headmaster in *The Observer*. These are not the precision and the flexibility desired.

the provision of stimulus to general 'extra-literary' reading. So much in his intellectual after-life may depend upon the start a man gets and the habits he forms at the university. And it is of the utmost importance that he should come on seminal and initiatory books that don't lie in his charted academic course. There should, then, be a specially accessible library containing (besides a great deal else) a number of copies of each of certain books, e.g. the best of Christopher Dawson, *Middletown*, Ian D. Suttie's *The Origins of Love and Hate*, and such works of sociology, anthropology, history, political thought, and so on, as might, after due consultation and consideration (and the library would be kept up to date) be picked on as appropriate. Some of them would be dealt with in discussion-group work. And some would be specified as likely to be referred to in the *viva* to be held at the end of the course. (The drawing-up and revision of the list would be a valuable experience for the seniors concerned.)

The capacity for a definitive reading of a book is a necessary qualification, and here may come a proposal designed to foster it. The review requirement already referred to would be extended outside the strictly literary-critical. The student would be required to produce a review of some book (the choice to be approved by authority) bearing on his Seventeenth-Century studies, and perhaps also of a book or two such as, though not directly related to a prescribed field, an educated man ought to be able to read, profit by and be articulate about.

It is time now to refer once again to the English Tripos as it now stands. In recognition of the sound principle that no one should be allowed to qualify for an Honours degree in the literature of his own language alone there is, obligatory for all candidates who have not studied another language than English in some other tripos, a paper in Part II called *French and Italian Set Books*. Candidates have merely to be prepared to translate passages from a number of specified texts—the list, it is true, is longish, and the student who prepares the whole will have done a good deal of miscellaneous and fragmentary reading. But no one who knows how in general practice the paper is prepared for, and how it is commonly regarded, will contend that it serves satisfactorily any respectable purpose. For it, then, would be substituted, to be undertaken by all candidates, firstly the study of Dante—a study designed to promote as good a knowledge and understanding of Dante as the conditions would allow.

This proposal has evoked the criticism that the conditions contemplated make it absurd: Dante is a large special study by himself. The argument, if admitted, would prove too much; we may as well abandon at once all thought of a humane education and the 'educated man,' and leave the multifarious specialists in 'humane' subjects to the functionless purity of their pure specialisms. Actually, Dante has not yet been formally jettisoned from our cultural heritage, and there is clearly no reason why the common assumption that educated people know something of him shouldn't, by work done in such a course as proposed, be honoured with a considerably more substantial grounding in actuality than it has. And there are obvious good reasons for making Dante a main study in such a course. It would involve, in a most effective kind of way, the study of a cultural order extremely different from that which has grown out of it—and which did grow out of it; and it would provide for the contemplation of the modern scene a measuring reference, and, in so far as such can ever be attained, a standing place, outside. This purpose, by reason of the complete contrast combined with direct historical relation, and the pregnant compactness of the field, it serves better than the study of Athenian civilization (about which our student might be presumed to know a good deal) prescribed in the Experimental College could serve it. The exploitable value of the Dante study in relation to the Seventeenth Century was intimated when that century was described as being in touch with 'the world of Dante.'

There is no French Dante. But clearly there should be some provision for giving effect to what may be assumed to be the generally admitted principle that no one should be allowed an Honours degree in English who can't, or doesn't, read French freely and intelligently. The requirement to translate passages from specified texts certainly doesn't ensure this. Instead there would be the requirement to write during the course of studies, an essay that would entail sustained and intelligent reading in French. Students might, within limits, advice being to hand and authorization necessary, be allowed to choose their subjects. A man might, for instance, write on that line from Baudelaire which has become of special interest to the English reader of poetry since Mr. Eliot arrived. He couldn't, of course, write his essay without having read a great deal in French outside his main focus. And the man who, having done such a piece of work, shouldn't have got a start that would carry him on in a subsequent year-by-year improvement of his acquaintance with French literature certainly wouldn't have got it from work for the ordinary kind of academic test.

It may be well before closing to give a summary of the scheme rather like that which might appear in a *Student's Handbook*:

(1) Practical Criticism: a number of papers, to be taken at the end of the course. These are to provide the test of literary education and critical competence.

(2) The Seventeenth Century in England: four or

five 'pieces of work,' on subjects chosen according to the principles explained, to be done during the course.

(3) An essay, to be written during the course, on the process of change by which England of the Seventeenth Century turned into the England of to-day.

(4) Dante, a general study: a paper, or papers, to be taken at the end of the course.

(5) A subject from French literature or literary history: a substantial essay, to be written during the course.

(6) Reviews, to be written during the course, of a number of books which are to be chosen in consultation with authority.

(7) A *viva voce* examination to be held at the end of the course.

N.B.—Participation required in organized discussion- and seminar-work.

This, then, offered in the spirit indicated, is an answer to the interrogative form of acquiescence that criticism of the present system commonly meets with: 'Yes, it's very unsatisfactory, we all know that; but what would you put in its place?' A practical kind of answer? Yes, in the sense that, if an experiment on these lines were authorized and facilities were provided (as they *could* be), and those running it believed in it energetically, it could certainly be made successful. Is the existing system practical? one might ask. At any rate, what it amounts to in practice bears a pitifully remote relation to what it formally pretends to be.

The scheme proposed will, no doubt, in spite of the professed intention and spirit, be called Utopian. Yet that reforms are badly needed is commonly realized both by students and their seniors, and it is difficult to see how, except on some such lines, there can be any real reform. The attempted combination of different subjects in the manner discussed by Mr. E. W. F. Tomlin in his *Scrutiny of Modern Greats* [1]—subjects to be studied and examined on in the usual academic way—will not in practice produce anything like the comprehensive and balanced education intended. And the *Ersatz* discipline (or grind)—Anglo-Saxon, Latin, Semasiological or what—that is so widely favoured by the academic mind as a way of introducing a stiffening reality into the literary curriculum can only make things worse.

The concluding emphasis may fitly fall once more on the Idea of a University. The profit of experiment on the suggested lines is, as has already been insisted, not to be thought of merely in terms of a student-product to be turned out. The work of running the School, with the contacts and collaborations it would involve, would produce a focal centre in which the Idea of a University would be present and alive as it nowhere is now. The profit wouldn't be merely within the School of English; anyone thinking to compute it would have to look, not merely outside that School, but outside the business of humane education.

[1] See *Scrutiny*, Vol. IV, No. 4.

Chapter III

LITERARY STUDIES

WHEN the substance of the foregoing chapter appeared in *Scrutiny* a correspondent remarked on the
inconspicuousness in my *Sketch for an English School* of the
avowed central interest, literature, and suggested that I
should write further and explain my provisions for making
the other-than-literary work justify itself—demonstrate
its pertinence—in improved performance in the literary-
critical field: 'As it stands, the superficial censor might
say that [the scheme] seems to show more concern for
history.' In reply I gratefully took the opportunity of
stressing what I hope has been made quite plain here:
the point of the scheme was, I said, not that all this work
should be focussed on the production of the complete
literary critic, but that they should be qualified literary
critics who did such work—that it should be undertaken
by minds informed, sensitized and equipped in a thorough
literary training. What might, perhaps, fairly be demanded of me was some account of my Part I, which was
to provide for competence in literature.

I am not, however, now proposing to supply a formal
'sketch' that shall pair with the one just submitted. For
that 'sketch,' it will be recalled, was offered merely as a
compromise solution, and I don't want the compromise
aspect to be forgotten: the approach by way of 'Part'
belongs to that. The experimenters, it was assumed,
would be given for experiment only their Part II. The
student's earlier course would be outside their province,
though they were to count on his coming to them well-
qualified already in literature. If they had a free hand to

66

organize the whole course, the whole field of work, they would hardly proceed from such a division of it into literary and extra-literary. Nevertheless, though it is not in the plan to sketch as corollary to the revolutionized Part II an equally revolutionized Part I, there are things to be said about necessary changes in current practice; changes that would make possible a better use of the time, in any case limited, that can be allowed for work in literature.

The problem of getting done, in any allowance of time that can be thought of as assignable to it, the work necessary if the qualifications specified are to be really acquired will no doubt be insisted on by critics of the scheme. The student is to come to Part II bringing with him a good knowledge of English literature from Chaucer, trained perception and judgment, and a skilled habit of critical analysis and critical expression—a tall order, it will be said. Among those who say it most sceptically will certainly be some who haven't the good fortune to know with how good a start, even as things are, students can come up from school. And there is no conclusive reason why students in general who intend to read English should not come up with as good a start. But, of course, no general improvement can be expected in the schools until there has been an improvement at the university. We are back at the question: in what ways could time and energy be better spent there?

It must be said bluntly that as things are, even where enlightenment most prevails and literature is emancipated from linguistic, a bad economy is positively prescribed, and the student wastes his labour not only through lack of guidance, but in compliance with authoritative misdirection. Are the principles that should govern a School of English so hard to grasp? Here, to begin with, is a negative formulation: there is no more futile study than that which ends with mere knowledge *about* literature. If literature is worth study, then the test of its having been so will be the ability to read literature intelligently, and apart from this ability an accumulation of knowledge is so much lumber. The study of a literary text about which the student cannot say, or isn't concerned to be able to say, as a matter of first-hand perception and judgment—of intelligent realization—why it should be worth study is a self-stultifying occupation.

Even as a specialist business literary scholarship is apt to defeat even its own limited purpose through having neglected to provide itself with a minimum gleam of critical intelligence; and the English 'Honours' man who, dealing with Shakespeare, cannot show more competence as a reader of English poetry than is commonly evidenced by footnotes in (say) his *Arden* edition has certainly defeated the true purpose of the School responsible for his training. Literary history, as a matter of 'facts about' and accepted critical (or quasi-critical) description and commentary, is a worthless acquisition; worthless for the student who cannot as a critic—that is, as an intelligent and discerning reader—make a personal approach to the essential data of the literary historian, the works of literature (an approach is personal or it is nothing: you cannot take over the appreciation of a poem, and unappreciated, the poem isn't 'there'). The only acquisition of literary history having any educational value is that made in the exercise of critical intelligence to the ends of the literary critic. Does this need arguing? Yet I have known the 'outlines of literary history' proposed as part of a test that, taken early in the 'Honours' course, should determine whether or not the student should be allowed to proceed—proposed, that is, as a subject of preparatory study.

It is plain that in the work of a properly ordered English

68

School (and here we have the positive corollary of the negative proposition thrown out above) the training of reading capacity has first place. By training of reading capacity I mean the training of perception, judgment and analytic skill commonly referred to as 'practical criticism'—or, rather, the training that 'practical criticism' ought to be. Sureness of judgment, of course, implies width of experience, and there is an unending problem of adjusting, in the student's work, the relations of intensive to extensive. Nevertheless, 'practical criticism' has a certain obvious priority; otherwise the acquisition of experience will be (as it so often is) an illusory matter. With the gain in experience will go more advanced and extended applications of critical method that develop out of the limited initial work—more difficult and sustained exercises in the essential discipline.

Practical criticism, training of perception and judgment, analysis—what are these, or what can they be, to justify this stress laid on them, the key-function here assigned them, as discipline? That the question will be asked by some of those to whom my 'sketch' must be thought of as being addressed has now to be recognized, though there is no way of giving a convincing answer here to the most sceptical kind of asker. The only conceivably effective answer would be some fairly prolonged exemplification of relevant work as it would be carried on in routine practice. It is obviously impossible to produce in this note the substance of a manual of analytic method—and the book to send the reader to doesn't exist. That the problem of demonstration should arise as such brings home how little, in the way of performance of their function, is commonly expected, or to be expected, either of literary critics or of English Schools.

For surely, as one might say to one's beginning students, it should be possible, by cultivating attentive reading, to acquire a higher skill than the untrained reader has: a skill that will enable the trained reader to do more with a poem than ejaculate approval or disapproval, or dismiss it with vaguely reported general impressions, qualified with the modest recognition that (in Arnold Bennett's words) 'taste after all is relative.' Analysis, one would go on, is the process by which we seek to attain a complete reading of the poem—a reading that approaches as nearly as possible to the perfect reading. There is about it nothing in the nature of 'murdering to dissect,' and suggestions that it can be anything in the nature of laboratory-method misrepresent it entirely. We can have the poem only by an inner kind of possession; it is 'there' for analysis only in so far as we are responding appropriately to the words on the page. In pointing to them (and there is nothing else to point to) what we are doing is to bring into sharp focus, in turn, this, that and the other detail, juncture or relation in our total response; or (since 'sharp focus' may be a misleading account of the kind of attention sometimes required), what we are doing is to dwell with a deliberate, considering responsiveness on this, that or the other node or focal point in the complete organization that the poem is, in so far as we have it. Analysis is not a dissection of something that is already and passively there. What we call analysis is, of course, a constructive or creative process. It is a more deliberate following-through of that process of creation in response to the poet's words which reading is. It is a re-creation in which, by a considering attentiveness, we ensure a more than ordinary faithfulness and completeness.

As addressed to other readers it is an appeal for corroboration; 'the poem builds up in this way, doesn't it? this bears such-and-such a relation to that, don't you agree?' In the work of an English School this aspect of mutual check—positively, of collaboration 'in the common pursuit of true judgment'—would assert itself as a matter of course.

To insist on this critical work as discipline is not to contemplate the elaboration of technical apparatus and drill. The training is to be one in the sensitive and scrupulous use of intelligence; to that end, such help as can be given the student will not be in the nature of initiations into technical procedures, and there is no apparatus to be handed over—a show of such in analytic work will most likely turn out to be a substitute for the use of intelligence upon the text. Where help can and should be got, of course, is in examples of good practice, wherever these can be found. 'Instruction' will take the form of varied and developing demonstration, offered to the actively critical student (i.e. in discussion-work conditions) as exemplifying a suitable use of intelligence.

And it is not only good examples that have an educational function. A useful exercise for the moderately seasoned student would be to go through W. Empson's *Seven Types of Ambiguity*, or parts of it, discriminating between the profitable and the unprofitable, the valid and the vicious. Empson's extremely mixed and uneven book, offering as it does a good deal of valuable stimulus, serves the better as a warning—a warning against temptations that the analyst whose practice is to be a discipline must resist. It abounds in instances of ingenuity that has taken the bit between its teeth. Valid analytic practice is a strengthening of the sense of relevance: scrutiny of the parts must be at the same time an effort towards fuller realization of the whole, and all appropriate play of intelligence, being also an exercise of the sense of value, is controlled by an implicit concern for a total value-judgment.

Another mixed provision of the stimulating and the aberrant that the student will inevitably come across and could with profit be helped to make some critical use of is the work of I. A. Richards. Here, of course, will be found the ambition to make analysis a laboratory technique, and the student going through *Practical Criticism* will note that nevertheless—or consequently—the show of actual analysis in that book is little more than show. The later 'semasiological' work, with its insistent campaign against the 'Proper (or One Right) Meaning Superstition' and its lack of any disciplinary counter-concern has tended, in so far as it has had influence, to encourage the Empsonian kind of irresponsibility. Inadequate and naïve ideas about the workings of language do without doubt prevail in the academic world and outside, and can profitably receive attention, but there will hardly have been profit on the balance if the literary student, as a result, tends to forget the one right total meaning that should commonly control his analysis.

If the dubious reader has by now some notion of what at any rate the literary critical discipline is not, that is something gained. To go very far in a positive account is not possible here, and by some readers (by most, perhaps, of those I shall actually have) will not be thought necessary. It will be gathered that demonstration and guidance even at the outset will take as little as possible the form, 'this is the correct method.' In the early stages, of course, there must be some pretty positive initiation. This would be done in terms of type-cases so elementary and obvious that the use they are put to could hardly be questioned by anyone of literary experience. Since so much stress has been laid on the 'discipline,' and since the assumption is that I am not addressing merely those who do not need convincing, I had better commit myself in a certain amount of detailed illustration. What follows is a compressed summary, such as might appear in a manual of critical analysis, of what might be done in discussion in a practical criticism group.[1]

One would take for a start a familiar piece, the nature and quality of which are immediately obvious—Arnold's sonnet *To Shakespeare* will do very well:

> Others abide our question. Thou art free.
> We ask and ask: Thou smilest and art still,
> Out-topping knowledge. For the loftiest hill
> That to the stars uncrowns his majesty,
> Planting his steadfast footsteps in the sea,
> Making the heaven of heavens his dwelling-place,
> Spares but the cloudy border of his base
> To the foil'd searching of mortality;
> And thou, who didst the stars and sunbeams know,
> Self-school'd, self-scann'd, self-honour'd, self-secure,
> Didst walk on earth unguess'd at. Better so!
> All pains the immortal spirit must endure,
>> All weakness that impairs, all griefs that bow,
>> Find their sole voice in that victorious brow.

That (one might preface) would not in the ordinary way challenge critical attention. It is the kind of thing that we recognize at a glance, place, and pass by, without stopping to analyse and examine—there is no need. Faced, there being no text to hand, with describing it for someone who chanced not to recollect it we might very well say (this description would probably emerge from the group), 'It's a sonnet in the Grand Style, in the Wordsworth-Milton manner.' And in saying this (one might go on to suggest) we should, for a moderately intelligent and experienced person, be conveying a strong presumption (which might just possibly be wrong) as to value—a strong presumption that nothing more need be said. It would be gathered that the sonnet is, in the

---

[1] It comes, as a matter of fact, from a book on analysis and appreciation not yet published.

pejorative sense, literary—a piece of mere versifying; a product of good taste at the best, and nothing more.

I am assuming now a general agreement about it to this effect. But the problem would be to work out how one might set about enforcing such a judgment if someone should question it. Matthew Arnold, after all, is a poet of repute and the sonnet may be found in the standard anthologies.

In criticism, of course (one would emphasize), nothing can be proved; there can, in the nature of the case, be no laboratory-demonstration or anything like it. Nevertheless, it is nearly always possible to go further than merely asserting a judgment or inviting agreement with a general account. Commonly one can call attention to this, that or the other detail by way of making the nature and force of one's judgment plain. And in a case as simple as the present one can very often, putting a finger on something in the text, make an observation that is irresistible and final.

In Matthew Arnold's sonnet (it would be concluded in discussion) such a place is clearly the fifth line:

Planting his steadfast footsteps in the sea . . .

The trope of a hill's 'planting its feet' in the sea would have passed: it is sanctioned currency, and in suggestion (such as it has) it is static. But 'footsteps' (arrived at through 'apt alliteration') introduces a ludicrous suggestion of gigantic, ponderously wading strides. Or rather, it would do so if the line were anything but a matter of words of no very particular effect. For clearly, it could only have been offered by an unrealizing mind, handling words from the outside. And if we ask how it is that any reader (as clearly many have done) lets it pass, the answer is that the sonnet imposes the kind of attention, or inattention, that it needs. It imposes an unrealizing

74

attention, if 'attention' is the word. The reader (the right one) yields himself deferentially, and responds with unction, to the familiar signals:

> Others abide our question. Thou art free.
> We ask and ask: Thou smilest and art still,
> Out-topping knowledge.

After that opening the critically-inert reader recognizes happily what he is being offered, and no one else has much hope. And, as a matter of fact, the whole sonnet turns out to be an orotund exercise in thuriferous phrases and generalities, without one touch of particularity or distinction. Arnold is not using a conventional Grand Style for the expression of a personally felt theme; he is using it, in the absence of anything to say, as a substitute; the vague prestige-value inhering in the phrases because of the work of other poets has to serve instead of meaning. Whatever he may suppose, he has nothing worth calling a theme. Had he realized in the least what purports to be his theme, Shakespeare's greatness or inscrutability, a mountain could never have presented itself to him as a symbol for it. There is nothing remote or austerely and inhumanly exalted about Shakespeare, whose genius is awe-inspiring by the inwardness and completeness of its humanity: it commands us from within. But to a versifier in the Romantic tradition (and a Wordsworthian) at that date, genuflecting poetically before a vague idea of poetic genius, the mountain would come inevitably—its massiveness a vague compensation, as it were, for the vagueness of the idea. So little is Arnold really concerned with Shakespeare (or anything in particular) that he can give us as one line of fourteen:

> And thou, who didst the stars and sunbeams know . . .

It would not be impressive, even if less irrelevant, addressed to Wordsworth; addressed to Shakespeare it is an unwitting confession of vacuity.

There is no need to examine the sonnet further here. One could make finally plain just how one intended to place it by saying that there are at any time at least half a dozen poets at Oxford or Cambridge who could write a poem as good. The reason for considering it at all was that it offers an obvious and very simple illustration of a point in critical method. Putting a finger on the 'steadfast footsteps' of the fifth line, one can show that what betrays itself indefensibly there is a general debility that is manifested throughout the sonnet in the dead conventionality of the phrasing—in the lack of any vital organization among the words. The unfortunate trope is the local index of a radical absence of grasp: the poet can only have committed it because he had nothing in particular that he was intent on realizing. Throwing out a practical tip for the analyst, one might add that general deficiency in the whole tends to betray itself locally in this way, and that, in verifying and enforcing a judgment, it is the metaphors and the imagery in especial that one should scrutinize for producible evidence.

Having said this, however, one draws back from making the tip more explicit. It is easy to point out that Matthew Arnold's metaphor is completely and betrayingly unrealized. But it will not do to say simply that in good poetry the metaphors are realized. In fact, there are hardly any rules that can, with any profit, be laid down: the best critical terms and concepts one can find or provide oneself with will be inadequate to the varied complexities with which the critic has to deal. Take, for instance, the idea of 'realization' that was introduced with 'realized' and 'unrealized'—terms that will be used again, for they are indispensable. Any suggestion that these terms introduce a simple or easily applied criterion may be countered with the following passage:

> All our service,
> In every point twice done, and then done double,
> Were poor and single business to contend
> Against those honours deep and broad wherewith
> Your majesty loads our house.
>
> [*Macbeth*, I, VI.]

This is an ordinary piece of mature Shakespeare. That is, without exemplifying the more remarkable Shakespearean complexity, it has the life and body which are the pervasive manifestation of Shakespeare's genius in his verse. The effect of concreteness—of being, we might say, 'realized' and not merely verbal—depends above all on the implicit metaphor introduced with 'deep and broad.' Those adjectives, plainly, describe a river, and, whether we tell ourselves so or not, the presence of a river makes itself felt in the effect of the passage, giving a physical quality to 'contend,' in the third line, that it would not otherwise have had. Prompted by 'honours' Shakespeare has, in the apprehensive rapidity of his mind, picked up the conventional trope of the king's being the 'fount of honour,' and, characteristically, in his rapid motion, brought it to life—its life, which is a matter of its organic relation to the context, being manifested in the very absence of explicitness. It is this absence of explicitness in the metaphor—of full realization, one might put it—that conditions the hardly noticeable shift to the metaphor of 'loads' in the next line: the common effect of being borne down by overwhelming profusion covers the shift. [Discussing the passage elsewhere,[1] I have observed that what we see as the inimitable mark of the poet in it is his ability to control realization to the precise degree appropriate in the given place—an ability that

[1] *How to Teach Reading :* see Appendix II, below.

clearly cannot be simulated if anything in the least metaphorically complex is offered.] One might, by way of emphasizing that 'realization' is not offered as a technical term, an instrument of precision, put it this way: it is in the incomplete realization of the metaphors that the realizing gift of the poet and the 'realized' quality of the passage are manifested. However we apply the term, what we have to consider is always a whole of some complexity: what we have to look for are the signs of something grasped and held, something presented in an ordering of words, and not merely thought of or gestured towards.

Nevertheless, it is still, by this account, local signs the critic should be looking for, this and that in the text to put his finger on in the hope of making an irresistible observation. And it holds that to tell him to scrutinize in particular the metaphor and imagery is to direct his attention the most likely way. But here it may seem that the question of definition properly comes up again. What is metaphor? What is imagery? I do not think that much profit is likely to come of trying to answer these questions directly, in general terms. What would be in place at this point would be a negative; a reminder, for dismissal, of a notion commonly held: it will not do to think of metaphor as compressed simile, simile being taken as a matter of illustrative correspondence—idea and image, main thought or theme and enlivening parallel.

For making so elementary a point the *Arden* editor's note on the 'dusty death' passage of *Macbeth* (Act V, Scene v) would provide a good opportunity. There is no room to deal with that note here. I will instead suggest how, after dealing with examples of the ostensibly simple simile that turns out to be something more complex, one might illustrate the wider bearings of this local analysis on method in Shakespeare criticism. A still greater complexity (one would point out) reveals itself when, reading the first speech in Act I, Scene VII of *Macbeth*, we stop at

> . . . pity, like a naked new-born babe . . .

and ask what kind of simile that is. Or rather, we might ask if we found the line (under Pity) in a dictionary of quotations. For actually, in reading the speech, we shouldn't stop at the end of the line, but go on at least to the next phrase,

> Striding the blast,

by when the effect would so have complicated itself that we should hardly start by commenting (as we might if the line stood by itself) that the 'naked new-born babe' is really not Pity, but the object of pity: the disturbing strangeness of

> a naked new-born babe
> Striding the blast

carries us on beyond such a consideration, and, indeed, away from 'pity.' In fact, the passage, in the movement and structure of its sense, forbids us to stop before the end of the sentence, three lines further on, by when it has become plain that 'pity,' whatever part it may play in the total effect, is certainly not at the centre—certainly doesn't represent the main significance. To bring out fully what this is it is necessary to quote the speech from the beginning:

> If it were done, when 'tis done, then 'twere well
> It were done quickly: if the assassination
> Could trammel up the consequence, and catch
> With his surcease success; that but this blow
> Might be the be-all and the end-all here,
> But here, upon this bank and shoal of time,
> We'd jump the life to come.—But in these cases,

We still have judgment here; that we but teach
Bloody instructions, which, being taught, return
To plague the inventor: this even-handed justice
Commends the ingredients of our poison'd chalice
To our own lips.   He's here in double trust:
First, as I am his kinsman and his subject,
Strong both against the deed; then, as his host,
Who should against his murderer shut the door,
Not bear the knife myself.   Besides, this Duncan
Hath borne his faculties so meek, hath been
So clear in his great office, that his virtues
Will plead like angels, trumpet-tongued, against
The deep damnation of his taking-off;
And pity, like a naked new-born babe,
Striding the blast, or heaven's cherubin, hors'd
Upon the sightless couriers of the air,
Shall blow the horrid deed in every eye,
That tears shall drown the wind.—I have no spur
To prick the sides of my intent, but only
Vaulting ambition, which o'erleaps itself
And falls on the other . . .

It is a speech that exhibits Shakespeare's specific genius
—an essentially poetic genius that is at the same time
essentially dramatic—at its most marvellous. The speech
is that of the intensely realized individual, Macbeth, at
the particular, intensely realized moment in the development of the poem. Analysis leads us directly to the core
of the drama, its central, animating interests, the principles of its life. The whole organism is present in the
part. Macbeth, weighing his hesitation, tells himself
that it is no moral or religious scruple, deriving its disturbing force from belief in supernatural sanctions. His
fear, he says, regards merely the chances of lasting
practical success in this world. His shrinking from the
murder expresses, he insists, a simple consideration of
expediency. Then he proceeds to enlarge on the peculiar
heinousness of murdering Duncan, and as he does so that
essential datum concerning his make-up, his ignorance

of himself, becomes plain. He supposes that he is developing the note of inexpediency, and picturing the atrocity of the crime as it will affect others. But already in the sentence invoking the sanctity of hospitality another note begins to prevail. And in the next sentence the speech achieves its unconscious self-confutation:

> Besides, this Duncan
> Hath borne his faculties so meek, hath been
> So clear in his great office, that his virtues
> Will plead like angels, trumpet-tongued, against
> The deep damnation of his taking-off;
> And pity, like a naked new-born babe,
> Striding the blast, or heaven's cherubin, hors'd
> Upon the sightless couriers of the air,
> Shall blow the horrid deed in every eye,
> That tears shall drown the wind.

The 'angels trumpet-tongued' (which is taken up in 'heaven's cherubin') and the 'deep damnation' (clearly expressing Macbeth's own innermost feelings) explain the uncanny oddity of

> pity, like a naked new-born babe,
> Striding the blast . . .

What we have in this passage is a conscience-tormented imagination, quick with terror of the supernatural, proclaiming a certitude that 'murder will out,' a certitude appalling to Macbeth not because of consequences on 'this bank and shoal of time,' but by reason of a sense of sin—the radical hold on him of religious sanctions. The 'pity' and the 'babe' carry on the 'meek,' combining to express Macbeth's horrified sense of the unforgivable heinousness of the murder. The vision that inspires the passage is not, though Macbeth (so maintaining a formal continuity from his initial cool self-deception to his imaginative self-exposure) suggests with his 'pity' that it is, the anticipated reaction of the multitudes whose 'tears shall drown the wind': it is a vision, dread and inescapable, of an outraged moral order vindicated by supernatural sanctions.[1]

The closing sentence—

> I have no spur
> To prick the sides of my intent, but only
> Vaulting ambition, which o'erleaps itself
> And falls on the other [side]

—provides useful illustrations for countering the unfortunate visual suggestion of 'image' and 'imagery'; for countering also too simple notions of 'exquisite unity of thought' (see the *Arden* editor's note on 'dusty death'). Macbeth's 'intent' of murder is, to his feeling, quite other than himself; as external to himself as an unwilling horse between his thighs; he can muster no impulse sharp enough to prick it into action. Then, with a rapid change in his psychological relation to the horse, he expresses the sense of difficulty and danger that produces this paralysis —a sense at the same time of the supreme effort required (he is gathered tense for vaulting—this point in the speech is a good instance of the expressive use of line division) and of the terrifying impossibility of making sure that the process once started can be stopped at the point of achievement in view.

Shakespeare, of course, has his own miraculous complexity. Nevertheless, the effects just examined serve in their striking way to enforce a general point. What we are concerned with in analysis are always matters of complex verbal organization; it will not do to treat

---

[1] Mr. Santayana seems to me guilty of an extraordinarily uncritical procedure (see *Tragic Philosophy*, *Scrutiny*, March, 1936) when he takes the ' To-morrow and to-morrow and to-morrow ' speech and opposes it, as if it were Shakespeare's own utterance or represented the total burden of the play, to Dante's

in la sua volontade è nostra pace.

metaphors, images and other local effects as if their relation to the poem were at all like that of plums to cake, or stones attesting that the jam is genuine. They are worth examining—they are there to examine—because they are foci of a complex life, and sometimes the context from which they cannot be even provisionally separated, if the examination is to be worth anything, is a wide one.

This should be enough to suggest how, in his study of Shakespeare and his use of Shakespeare criticism, the student's critical training would equip him for dealing with the aberrations of both Bradley and Wilson Knight. And (what was the main aim) perhaps enough positive illustration has by now been offered to preclude serious misunderstandings about what I mean by 'analysis,' to which I have assigned so important a place. Illustration of that kind takes up an inordinate amount of room; and I can only with the greatest brevity suggest representative exercises in which questions of value-judgment regarding emotional quality, and so on, would be raised. There is the type-contrast between Scott's *Proud Maisie* and Cory's *Heraclitus* (542 and 759 in the *Oxford Book*—556 and 768 in the new edition)—the contrast between the poem that seems to state and present barely without emotional comment, the emotion being generated between the parts when the reader has them in his mind, and the poem that is overtly emotional and incites directly to a 'moved' response, the emotion seeming to lie out there on the page. That *Heraclitus* is sentimental is a judgment that can be enforced. Of Tennyson's *Break! break! break!* one wouldn't say this, but certain dangers attending its mode of emotional expression will come up for discussion when the poem in its turn is contrasted with Wordsworth's *A slumber did my spirit seal*. Again, in a related contrast, the superiority of D. H. Lawrence's *Piano* (Poem VIII in

I. A. Richards's *Practical Criticism*) over *Tears, idle tears,* can be demonstrated in analysis.

Demonstration of the inferiority of Hood's *Autumn* to the poems of Keats from which it derives makes a good approach to the critical study of Keats himself. And with this work might go analytic comparison of characteristic Keatsian verse with (say) Shelleyan and Tennysonian, done explicitly as an induction into the intelligent general reading of all three poets and as an indication how the fuller critique, the comprehensive evaluating description, should be developed. The point I am trying to make here is one of general application: it is that the time-honoured academic way of telling a student to write his essay on 'Wordsworth's thought' or 'Shelley the poet of the revolutionary creed' or 'Tennyson and Victorian doubt,' and leaving him to the poet's collected works and the guidance of Oliver Elton or the equivalent (including the usual lectures), means an enormous waste of time and spirit. Without a trained reading capacity he cannot profitably attempt the vast and speedy consumption of the printed word nominally expected of him, and examination tests designed to ensure that, untrained, he shall 'really have read the actual authors' are futile. But with a trained eye, a critical equipment and knowledge of how to approach he can explore, and read extensively, with decidedly more profit than most of the recommended authorities would seem to have brought from their perusals.

Consider again how much time the literary student is usually expected to devote to Elizabethan and Jacobean drama, and how little is done to help him to acquire a relevant critical equipment. Not only does he need to be intelligent about dramatic verse, he needs to be intelligent too about dramatic conventions and the possibilities of poetic drama—intelligent as only well-directed discussion can be expected to make him. Such discussion would

make good use of the appropriate places in Mr. Eliot's
critical writings, and would result in the student's being
able to bring to bear on his Elizabethan reading some
knowledge of Greek drama and a familiarity with Mr.
Eliot's own experiments. No amount of scholarship about
Pre-Shakespearean drama can be a valuable substitute
for this informed intelligence, nor can the ability to
summarize the plots of Beaumont and Fletcher. Critically equipped, on the other hand, he has a use for scholarship and can read widely with unfeigned interest and
educational advantage.

Academic practice does, of course, prescribe a study of
literary criticism; but though in the prescribed reading
the student will find drama referred to a good deal, he
will not find the equipment he needs, or much help
towards acquiring it. For surely we can generalize and
say that the student's dealings with literary criticism
('History and Theory,' or whatever the heading may be)
should have for first, chief and essential aim to increase
his efficiency as a reader and critic of poems, novels and
plays—to improve his qualifications for tackling his
crowded intellectual programme. But can anyone suppose that if this had been the operative principle Aristotle,
Longinus, Sidney, Dryden, Addison and the rest would
have had, in the curriculum and on the examination
paper, the place they have? To say that they 'raise all
the questions' is obtuse and disingenuous: a man may
get high marks on them and remain utterly unqualified
for intelligent reading, and no study of them as they are
offered is likely to improve anyone's ability to read works
of literature, or think about them. The student does
indeed need a critical equipment if he is not to waste his
time, and he must take it *to* the prescribed critics if he is
to profit by them at all.

His essential equipment he must acquire in directed

discussion of the main critical questions as they come up in practical criticism and are raised in T. S. Eliot's critical work, and here and there in places that the qualified director of discussion will know of. Once the student has formed for himself a criterion of intelligent critical thinking and knows what really saying anything about a work of literature looks like, he will be able to improve his equipment in the course of his incidental reading of what good criticism there is.[1] And he will also be able to read without waste Aristotle, Johnson, Coleridge and Arnold and acquire without difficulty what of the 'History of Literary Criticism' may be worth having. As things are, he is not only denied what he needs; he is made to spend himself and blunt his edge on dutiful and unrewarding rote-work (unrewarding except in examination-room profit—you memorize what, prompted by lecturers and other authorities, the good student knows he ought to find in the text).

Illustrations could be multiplied, but perhaps the point has been sufficiently enforced: the student could use his time with very much greater advantage than academic requirements and academic defaults now permit, even in the most enlightened of English Schools. And, unless he is one of those who oughtn't in any case to be reading for Honours in English, it is not extravagant to count on his acquiring competence in literature as postulated in my 'sketch.'

[1] See below, pp. 121 and 132, and also the Note to Page 121, at the end of Appendix II.

Appendix I

T. S. ELIOT'S LATER POETRY

THE Dry Salvages ('pronounced to rhyme with *assuages*') is the third member to appear of a sequence that began with *Burnt Norton*, continued with *East Coker*, and, one gathers, is to be completed in a fourth poem. Each member is a poem in itself, as the separate publication intimates, but it is plain now, with three of the four to hand, that the sequence is to be a real whole; a total context which each constituent poem needs for its full significance. Now, too, with this new poem before him, the literary critic finds himself once more turning over the principle that poetry is to be judged as poetry—turning it over and wondering what it is worth and how far it will take him. May there perhaps be a point at which literary criticism, if (as he must believe) there is, or ought to be, such a thing, finds itself confronting the challenge to leave itself behind and become another thing? Is, in any case, the field of literary criticism so delimitable as to exempt him from the theological equipment he can lay no claim to?

In overcoming this last uneasiness he will have found encouragement in the performances of commentators who have not needed to share it: it will have been so clear that their advantage has not been altogether an advantage, but has tended to disqualify them for appreciating the nature of the poet's genius. They are apt to show too great an alacrity in response; to defeat his essential method by jumping in too easily and too happily with familiar terms and concepts. This is the method that is carried to an experimental (and hardly successful) extreme in *Family Reunion*, where, if I understand rightly, Mr. Eliot

87

aims at bringing his public, assumed for the purpose to be pagan, face to face with the Christian position or view of life without invoking Christian dogma, or such familiar concepts and symbols as would fall comfortably in with the lethargy of custom. In the poetry, of course, there is no pretence that the sensibility is not Christian; but it is not for nothing that D. W. Harding [1] described *Burnt Norton*, which doesn't stand apart from the body of Eliot's religious verse, as being concerned with the creation of concepts. The poet's magnificent intelligence is devoted to keeping as close as possible to the concrete of sensation, emotion and perception. Though this poetry is plainly metaphysical in preoccupation, it is as much poetry, it belongs as purely to the realm of sensibility, and has in it as little of the abstract and general of discursive prose, as any poetry that was ever written. Familiar terms and concepts are inevitably in sight, but what is distinctive about the poet's method is the subtle and resourceful discipline of continence with which, in its exploration of experience, it approaches them.

Of course, the sensibility being Christian, they lie behind the poetry, as well as being in front of it (so to speak) as something to be re-created; but they are never taken up as accepted instruments for getting to work with. We might apply here some adaptation of the poet's critical dictum: '(Tradition) cannot be inherited, and if you want it you must obtain it by great labour.' Well-equipped commentators would do well, for a simple illustration of the kind of dangers and temptations awaiting them, to consider how Eliot uses Dante in *Ash-Wednesday*, and how easy it would be with the aid of a Dante primer to work out an illuminating commentary that would

[1] See his extraordinarily interesting and penetrating review of *Collected Poems, 1908-1935*, in *Scrutiny* for September, 1936. It seems to me pre-eminently the note on Eliot to send people to.

save grateful readers the trouble of understanding the poem.

The poetry from *Ash-Wednesday* onwards doesn't say, 'I believe,' or 'I know,' or 'Here is the truth'; it is positive in direction but not positive in that way (the difference from Dante is extreme). It is a searching of experience, a spiritual discipline, a technique for sincerity—for giving 'sincerity' a meaning. The preoccupation is with establishing from among the illusions, evanescences and unrealities of life in time an apprehension of an assured reality—a reality that, though necessarily apprehended in time, is not of it. There is a sustained positive effort—the constructive effort to be 'conscious':

> Time past and time future
> Allow but a little consciousness.
> To be conscious is not to be in time
> But only in time can the moment in the rose-garden.
> The moment in the arbour where the rain beat,
> The moment in the draughty church at smokefall
> Be remembered; involved with past and future.
> Only through time time is conquered.
>
> *Burnt Norton.*

With these 'moments' is associated 'the sudden illumination':

> The moments of happiness—not the sense of well-being,
> Fruition, fulfilment, security or affection,
> Or even a very good dinner, but the sudden illumination—
> We had the experience, but missed the meaning,
> And approach to the meaning restores the experience
> In a different form, beyond any meaning
> We can assign to happiness.
>
> *The Dry Salvages.*

'Illumination,' it will be seen, is no simple matter, and *Ash-Wednesday*, where the religious bent has so pronounced a liturgical expression, is remarkable for the insistent and subtle scrupulousness of the concern manifested to guard against the possibilities of temptation, self-deception and confusion that attend on the aim and the method.

Perhaps the way in which the sense of an apprehended higher reality, not subject to the laws of time and mundane things, is conveyed is most simply illustrated in *Marina*, that lovely poem (a limiting description) with the epigraph from Seneca. There, in the opening, the enchanted sense of a landfall in a newly discovered world blends with the suggestions (to be taken up later on in the poem) of 'daughter'—the 'daughter' being associated by the title of the poem with the Shakespearean heroine who, lost at sea, was miraculously found again, for the father an unhoped-for victory over death:

> What seas what shores what grey rocks and what islands
> What water lapping the bow
> And scent of pine and the woodthrush singing through the
> fog
> What images return
> O my daughter.

The images that follow in the next paragraph bring in the insistently recurring 'Death' after each line, and they are evoked in order that we may find that they now

> Are become unsubstantial, reduced by a wind,
> A breath of pine, and the woodsong fog
> By this grace dissolved in place.

It may be remarked that the mundane actuality, the world of inescapable death, is elsewhere in the poems of the phase less easily dismissed; its reduction to unreality is a different affair, having nothing of enchantment about it, and the unreality is not absence. And perhaps it should be noted too as an associated point that 'grace,' in its equivocal way, is the one explicitly religious touch in *Marina*.

The evocation of the apprehended reality is now taken up, and is characteristic in method:

What is this face, less clear and clearer
The pulse in the arm, less strong and stronger—
Given or lent? more distant than stars and nearer than the
    eye

Whispers and small laughter between leaves and hurrying
    feet
Under sleep, where all the waters meet.

The face, 'less clear and clearer,' doesn't belong to the ordinary experience of life in time, and the effect of a higher reality is reinforced by the associations of the last two lines—associations that, with their potent suggestion, characteristic of some memories of childhood, of a supremely illuminating significance, recur so much in Eliot's later work:

We had the experience, but missed the meaning
And approach to the meaning restores the significance
In a different form, beyond any meaning
We can assign to happiness.

The effect depends upon a kind of co-operative co-presence of the different elements of suggestion, the co-operation being, as the spare and non-logical pointing intimates, essentially implicit, and not a matter for explicit development. What in fact we have is nothing of the order of affirmation or statement, but a kind of tentatively defining exploration.

The rest of the poem adds to the co-present elements the suggestion of a constructive effort, which, though what it constructs is defective and insecure, has a necessary part in the discovery or apprehension:

I made this . . .

    .   .   .   .
Made this unknowing, half-conscious, unknown, my own,
The garboard strake leaks, the seams need caulking.

This form, this face, this life
Living to live in a world of time beyond me; let me
Resign my life for this life, my speech for that unspoken,
The awakened, lips parted, the hope, the new ships.

Thus, in the gliding from one image, evocation or suggestion to another, so that all contribute to a total effect, there is created a sense of a supreme significance, elusive, but not, like the message of death, illusory; an opening into a new and more than personal life.

In the *Coriolan* poems it is the unreal actuality that fills the foreground of attention. They deal with the world of public affairs and politics, and it seems natural to call them satires; they are certainly great poetry, and they come as near to great satiric poetry as this age is likely to see Again we have a search for the real among temporal unrealities. *Triumphal March* gives us the great occasion, the public event, the supremely significant moment. The reduction and deflation of the 'significance' is effected by sudden uncommented slides of the focus, or shiftings of the plane. In the opening we share the exaltation and expectancy of the holiday crowd:

Stone, bronze, stone, steel, stone, oakleaves, horses' heels
Over the paving.
And the flags. And the trumpets. And so many eagles.
How many? Count them. And such a press of people.
We hardly knew ourselves that day, or knew the City.
This is the way to the temple, and we so many crowding
    the way.
So many waiting, how many waiting? what did it matter,
    on such a day?
Are they coming? No, not yet. You can see some eagles.
    And hear the trumpets.
Here they come. Is he coming?
The natural wakeful life of our Ego is a perceiving.
We can wait with our stools and our sausages.

In the last two lines we have two shifts; first to the level of philosophical observation,

T. S. ELIOT'S LATER POETRY

The natural wakeful life of our Ego is a perceiving

(which has its quasi-musical response towards the end of the poem in

> That is all we could see, etc.),

and then to the mob's natural level of banality (a theme developed in the final paragraph just referred to). Then again we have the tense expectancy; at last the real thing is about to appear:

> What comes first? Can you see? Tell us. It is
>
> > 5,800,000 rifles and carbines,
> > 102,000 machine guns,
> > 28,000 trench mortars   etc.

And it is at any rate one kind of basic 'reality' that, with ironical effect, the prolonged inhuman inventory gives us. That is what 'comes first,' contrasting significantly with the Lord Mayor's Show passage that takes it up at the level of 'human interest.' Following the Mayor and the Liverymen comes—supreme public moment, climax of the day—the Hero, the Führer, presented in a guise of equivocally godlike self-sufficiency:

> There is no interrogation in his eyes
> Or in the hands, quiet over the horse's neck,
> And the eyes watchful, waiting, perceiving, indifferent.

Comment follows immediately in the sudden shift to the imagery of 'consciousness'; imagery that evokes the eternal reality and the escape from time and the flux, and, recurrent as it is in the later poems, indicates the place among them of these satires as something like movements of one work:

> O hidden under the dove's wing, hidden in the turtle's
>   breast,
> Under the palmtree at noon, under the running water
> At the still point of the turning world. O hidden.

93

Difficulties of a Statesman works in the same way as *Triumphal March*. Dealing with the unrealities of politics and public affairs, the conventional importances, the loss of ends in the bustle of getting things done, the usurping and frustrating complication of the machinery—

> The first thing to do is to form the committees:
> The consultative councils, the standing committees, select committees and sub-committees.
> One secretary will do for several committees

—it places all this by the same kind of abrupt passing invocation of the eternal and ultimate, source of significance and peace. It ends with the consummate ironic duplicity of

RESIGN RESIGN RESIGN.

Burnt Norton, the first poem of the sequence to which *The Dry Salvages* belongs, has the effect of being in a special sense a 'fresh start.'[1] It is as if the poet were conducting a radical inquiry into the nature and methods of his exploration. The poem is as purely and essentially a poem as anything else of Mr. Eliot's; but it seems to me to be the equivalent in poetry of a philosophical work—to do by strictly poetical means the business of an epistemological and metaphysical inquiry. Of course, in this given case examination of the instruments is necessarily at the same time a use of them in the poet's characteristic kind of exploration. Yet to convey the distinctive character of this poem the stress must fall as I have suggested. Harding, in the illuminating commentary referred to above,

---

[1] So here I am, in the middle way, having had twenty years—
Twenty years largely wasted, the years of *l'entre deux guerres*—
Trying to learn to use words, and every attempt
Is a wholly new start . . .
                                        East Coker.

94

registers this character in his own way when he speaks of the poem as being concerned with the 'creation of concepts.'

The kind of expository generality that distinguishes *Burnt Norton* is well illustrated by the opening:

> Time present and time past
> Are both perhaps present in time future,
> And time future contained in time past.
> If all time is eternally present
> All time is unredeemable.
> What might have been is an abstraction
> Remaining a perpetual possibility
> Only in a world of speculation.
> What might have been and what has been
> Point to one end, which is always present.
> Footfalls echo in the memory
> Down the passage which we did not take
> Towards the door we never opened
> Into the rose-garden.   My words echo
> Thus, in your mind.

The general propositions of the first ten lines have, by the time we have read the rest of the passage, become clearly part of a *procédé* and a total effect that belong to poetry, and not to the order of abstraction of discursive prose. The particular memory evoked is not an illustration of the general propositions; these, rather, represent a pondering, with results in generalized significance, of the memory, the 'illuminative' quality of which, along with the unseizableness—

> the sudden illumination—
> We had the experience, but missed the meaning,
> And approach to the meaning restores the experience
> In a different form

—is marvellously conveyed.   The unseizableness—the specific indeterminate status of the experience and the elusiveness of the meaning—we can see being defined, or created, in the paradoxical

> Footfalls echo in the memory
> Down the passage which we did not take
> Towards the door we never opened
> Into the rose-garden.

'Footfalls echo' is a fact, and 'memory' becomes the 'passage' which, though we did not take it, is thus itself a present fact.

The complex effect of a de-realizing of the routine commonsense world together with the evoking of a reality that lies hidden among the unrealities into which life in time, closely questioned, paradoxes itself is clinched by the sudden shift:

> My words echo
> Thus, in your mind.

The 'not' and 'never' of the preceding sentence are 'thus' (finely placed word) in a way countered. To convey the status of what is apprehended, what stands, in this searching of experience takes both 'is' and 'is not.' The effect is completed by the disjoined next sentence—

> But to what purpose
> Disturbing the dust on a bowl of rose-leaves
> I do not know

—which, in its sudden drop to another plane, to a distancing comment, brings out by contrast the immediacy of what goes before, while at the same time contributing directly to the sensuous presentness of the whole—the words that echo 'thus' disturb, in front of us, 'the dust on a bowl of rose-leaves' ('dust' and 'rose-leaves' together evoke one of those co-presences of opposing associations which seem to replace words by immediate sensation, and the whole sentence, of course, relates back with various subtleties of significance to the 'rose-garden' and 'time' of the opening paragraph).

The re-creation of, or by, 'echoes'—

> other echoes
> Inhabit the garden

(and they are echoes that recur in *Family Reunion* as well as the poems), the restoring 'approach to the meaning,' continues in a sustained way in the remainder of the section, concluding with, for my 'unseizable,'

> Go, go, go, said the bird: human kind
> Cannot bear very much reality.

Regarding this reality we read in the next section:

> Yet the enchainment of past and future
> Woven in the weakness of the changing body,
> Protects mankind from heaven and damnation
> Which flesh cannot endure.

—The reality is sought because, by providing an absolute reference, it is to confront the spirit with the necessity of supreme decisions, ultimate choices, and so give a meaning to life; something not to be found in this 'place of disaffection' (which, plainly in this poetry, the spirit cannot endure) where

> Only a flicker
> Over the strained time-ridden faces
> Distracted from distraction by distraction
> Filled with fancies and empty of meaning
> Tumid apathy with no concentration
> Men and bits of paper, whirled by the cold wind
> That blows before and after time,
> Wind in and out of unwholesome lungs
> Time before and time after.
> Eructation of unhealthy souls
> Into the faded air, the torpid
> Driven on the wind that sweeps the gloomy hills of London,
> Hampstead and Clerkenwell, Campden and Putney,

97

> Highgate, Primrose and Ludgate.   Not here
> Not here the darkness, in this twittering world.

Burnt Norton develops the specifically religious note no further than the passages quoted above suggest.   What is characteristic of the poem is the sustained and marvellously resourceful preoccupation that Harding examines; the preoccupation with re-creating the concept of 'eternity.'

East Coker is at the other extreme from *Burnt Norton*: it is personal,[1] running even to autobiography (it is the most directly personal poem of Eliot's we have), and historical. We find ourselves (rightly or wrongly) relating its prevailing mood to Munich and the valedictory editorial of *The Criterion*.   It is written, with a passing resurgence of the 'echoes,' those reminders of the possibility of 'consciousness'—

> Whisper of running streams, and winter lightning,
> The wild thyme unseen and the wild strawberry,
> The laughter in the garden, echoed ecstasy
> Not lost, but requiring, pointing to the agony
> Of death and birth,

from 'the waste sad time' of the concluding two lines of *Burnt Norton*:

> Ridiculous the waste sad time
> Stretching before and after.

It is a discipline of meditation the note of which is:

> I said to my soul, be still, and wait without hope
> For hope would be hope for the wrong thing;   wait without
>   love
> For love would be love of the wrong thing; there is yet faith
> But the faith and the love and the hope are all in the
>   waiting.

[1] Mr. Eliot, I think, would object to this way of putting it, but I don't know how to indicate the distinctive quality of the poem without using the adjective.

T. S. ELIOT'S LATER POETRY

One section (IV) is a formal and traditional religious poem. The opening section, developing a note of family history, evokes historical time and change and the decay of the old organic culture. The last, starting with a passage of direct autobiography, develops the accompanying reflections and concludes with an inversion, *In my end is my beginning*, of the opening phrase of the whole poem.

The Dry Salvages hasn't the personal and historical qualities of *East Coker*; nor has it the abstract generality (for, in spite of the easy way in which we commonly oppose it to 'concrete,' 'abstract' seems the right word) of *Burnt Norton*. In its prevailing mode it lies between the other two poems. It is concerned mainly, not with the 'creation of concepts,' but with dissolving the habit-created 'reality' of routine experience and commonsense, with their protective (and constructive) anaesthesias. The genius of the poet[1] strikes us afresh in the opening section as,

---

[1] The extraordinary vitality of language in which the specifically poetic genius is so apparent gets, of course, nothing like representative attention in this review. It is apparent everywhere in the marvellous mastery of rhythm. For a random instance of the metaphorical life take, in the following passage, the characteristic ' shuttered '—a good instance of a metaphor that depends obviously on an element of *unlikeness*, of contrasting suggestion (some of the associations of ' shuttered room '), for its evocative strength :

> Now the light falls
> Across the open field, leaving the deep lane
> Shuttered with branches, dark in the afternoon . . .
>
> *East Coker*.

Another characteristic manifestation of the genius is this, from the same poem :

> Dawn points, and another day
> Prepares for heat and silence.

The ' points ' clearly comes from the French (*poindre* and *point du jour*). It is a *trouvaille* because of the suggestion, so felicitous in the context, of the regularly punctuating recurrences of time. Another,

subtly and inevitably, the symbolic significance of the 'river'—

> reminder
> Of what men choose to forget,

and of the sea—

> The river is within us, the sea is all about us,

emerge and are developed. The mind is made to feel how precariously it resists a lapsing away into the flux of the unknown and alien within; our environment of familiarities and certainties dissolves into a daunting indeterminateness of shifting perspectives and recessions. Human experience seems meaningless and vain in its relativity. Our sense and notion of time are unsettled into convicted arbitrariness and vanity by the evocation of times other than human and historical:

> . . . time not our time, rung by the unhurried
> Ground swell, a time
> Older than the time of chronometers, older
> Than time counted by anxious worried women
> Lying awake, calculating the future . . .

The subtlety of resource with which the sapping and

---

and equally characteristic, kind of effect is the creative play on ' still ' in these passages from *Burnt Norton* :

> After the kingfisher's wing
> Has answered light to light, and is silent, the light is still
> At the still point of the turning world.

> Only by the form, the pattern,
> Can words or music reach
> The stillness, as a Chinese jar still
> Moves perpetually in its stillness.
> Not the stillness of the violin, while the note lasts,
> Not that only . . .

Here the consummate management of stress and verse-movement is illustrated too.

unsettling are effected is complementary to the constructive subtlety analysed by Harding in *Burnt Norton*.

The day-to-day actuality of life in time, when we are restored to it in the second section, the inertia of human continuance, presents itself in its most desolating aspect as 'To-morrow and to-morrow and to-morrow'—

> There is no end, but addition: the trailing
> Consequence of further days and hours . . .

It is against this background that we have the reminder of the 'moments of happiness . . . the sudden illumination' that promise a release from the no-meaning of time:

> I have said before
> That the past experience revived in the meaning
> Is not the experience of one life only
> But of many generations . . .

There follow, in the close of the section, new subtleties in the symbolic use of the 'river' and the 'sea.' The third section develops the paradoxes of time and change, and the fourth is a formally Christian invocation. It is in the last section that there comes the culminating move to which the varied process of constructive exploration, with its accompaniments of negation and rejection, its indirections and strategic envelopments, has been leading up. The passage has behind it—is meant to be read with a full sense of its having behind it—what has gone before in the complex whole that begins with *Burnt Norton* (to take that as the relevant 'fresh start'). It is introduced immediately by a final preparatory negative, an admirably and characteristically dry dismissal of the usual traffic in the 'supernormal':

> To explore the womb, or tomb, or dreams; all these are
>   usual
> Pastimes and drugs, and features of the press:
> And always will be, some of them especially

When there is distress of nations and perplexity
Whether on the shores of Asia, or in the Edgware Road.
Men's curiosity searches past and future
And clings to that dimension.   But to apprehend
The point of intersection of the timeless
With time, is an occupation for the saint—
No occupation either, but something given
And taken, in a lifetime's death in love,
Ardour and selflessness and self-surrender.
For most of us, there is only the unattended
Moment, the moment in and out of time,
The distraction fit, lost in a shaft of sunlight,
The wild thyme unseen, or the winter lightning
Or the waterfall, or music heard so deeply
That it is not heard at all, but you are the music
While the music lasts.   These are only hints and guesses,
Hints followed by guesses; and the rest
Is prayer, observance, discipline, thought and action.
The hint half guessed, the gift half understood, is Incarna-
        tion.
Here the impossible union
Of spheres of existence is actual.

For the reader who comes charged with doctrine and
acceptance the term 'Incarnation' thus introduced will of
course have a greater potency than for another.   But in
that, as I have suggested at the beginning of this review,
he will not, for the appreciation of the poetry and of the
genius of the poet, be altogether at an advantage.   This
poetry, in its 're-creation of concepts,' is at the same time,
and inseparably, preoccupied with the nature of acceptance and belief; one might, in fact, say, adapting Harding, that to take the place of the words 'acceptance' and
'belief' is its essential aim.

The hint half guessed, the gift half understood, is Incarna-
        tion.
Here the impossible union
Of spheres of existence is actual

—these are, no doubt, statements, to be taken as such;

but though they imply a theological context, their actual context is the poem. It would be absurd to contend that the passage is not an invitation to a relating of the two contexts, but nothing is gained from the point of view of either poetry or religion by an abandonment of one context for the other, or by any approach that refuses or ignores or relaxes the peculiar discipline that the poetry is. And the critic can hardly insist too much that this affirmation which seems to strain forward out of the poem must, by the reader of the poem, be referred back to what has gone before. And he who doesn't read the poem ignores the poet's genius even while applauding. There is no reason why he shouldn't applaud too Miss Sayers' demonstrations of what the creative mind, on its mettle, can do for orthodoxy.

That the poetry seems to invite a given intellectual and doctrinal frame may be found to recommend it. But the frame is another thing (and the prose is not the poetry—Eliot himself has made some relevant observations). The genius, that of a great poet, manifests itself in a profound and acute apprehension of the difficulties of his age. Those difficulties are such that they certainly cannot be met by any simple reimposition of traditional frames. Eliot is known as professing Anglo-Catholicism and classicism; but his poetry is remarkable for the extraordinary resource, penetration and stamina with which it makes its explorations into the concrete actualities of experience below the conceptual currency; into the life that must be the *raison d'être* of any frame—while there is life at all. With all its positive aspiration and movement, it is at the same time essentially a work of radical analysis and revision, endlessly insistent in its care not to confuse the frame with the living reality, and heroic in its refusal to accept. In any case, to feel an immense indebtedness to Eliot, and to recognize the immense indebtedness of the age, one doesn't need to share his intellectually formulated conclusions, his doctrinal views, or even to be uncritical of the attitudes of his poetry.

To have gone seriously into the poetry is to have had a quickening insight into the nature of thought and language; a discipline of intelligence and sensibility calculated to promote, if any could, real vitality and precision of thought; an education intellectual, emotional and moral. From such a study it would be impossible to come away with a crudely simplifying attitude towards the problems facing the modern world, or without an enhanced consciousness of the need both for continuity and for 'fresh starts.' As remarked above, Eliot's work is peculiarly relevant to the stresses of our time; and this remains true, in spite of the change of fashions that set in at the beginning of the last decade. His relative distinction and his title to respect and gratitude are certainly not less than they were a dozen years ago. To him, in fact, might be adapted the tribute that he once paid to that very different genius, D. H. Lawrence; he preeminently has stood for the spirit in these brutal and discouraging years. And it should by now be impossible to doubt that he is among the greatest poets of the English language.

NOTE.—The above was written before the appearance of *Little Gidding*, the last member of the sequence. I record this merely in order to explain the absence of any reference to that poem. And I take the occasion to add that D. W. Harding wrote in *Scrutiny* for Spring, 1943, a review of *Little Gidding* that I find intensely interesting.

HOW TO TEACH READING

Part I: Critical of Mr. Pound

THE PLIGHT OF THE CULTIVATED

MR. Ezra Pound's pamphlet, *How to Read*, has, one hopes, been widely read. One may quarrel with it, but that is its value: it is a thing to quarrel with. Some such challenge was badly needed. It is a challenge to a stocktaking that has long been overdue, to a radical inquiry into the state of literary culture, and the questions it presses home need answering. What is the function of literary culture—its *raison d'être*? Why do we read, and why should we? By what standards, what criteria, what principles can we bring order into our reading (in so far as it doesn't belong with smoking) and establish it safely as something other than elegantly virtuous dissipation or (what is much the same thing) accumulation?

The plight that Mr. Pound, wittingly or unwittingly, forces us to contemplate is absurd and disastrous. Think of the range and variety of literature in which the cultivated modern must pretend to be at home. It is assumed, of course, that he is familiar with the classics, major and minor—and they are, in conventional acceptance, many —of his own tongue. Then there are *the* Classics. Homer, Aeschylus, Sophocles, Euripides, Theocritus, Virgil, Ovid, Catullus, Lucretius, Petronius, Apuleius and the rest he has, of course, all at command, properly placed, so that the allusions to them come and go easily. Not that he

FOOTNOTES.—Footnotes, or parts of footnotes, added in the revision of the original pamphlet are enclosed in square brackets.

need ever try to say anything about any of these; it is the current 'culture'-values that must be taken seriously: Joyce, Proust, Lawrence, Eliot, W. H. Auden (now that E. E. Cummings has gone out), Faulkner (succeeding to Hemingway), Valéry, Gide, Eluard, St.-J. Perse and a wide varying fringe. Apart from the *chic* contemporary names, one knows, of course, French literature in general and certain high currency-values in particular: Rimbaud, Laforgue, Corbière, Baudelaire. . . . And the Russians are not yet forgotten. Then there is Dante, whom one hasn't merely read, as one has Goethe and Lucretius (for one has, of course, read Santayana's *Three Philosophical Poets*).

The list is long. Some of the authors are difficult and some voluminous, so that, even if there weren't Einstein, Freud, Frazer, Trotsky, Eddington, Whitehead and a score of others, besides art and music, to be conversable about, Mr. Wyndham Lewis to keep up with, and the contemporary output to sift, reading what one is supposed to have read would be a full-time business.

THE DECAY OF THE COMMON READER

And it is not merely the amount that is the trouble; there is the heterogeneity. The acquiring of taste is probably more difficult to-day than it ever was before. Consider for contrast the eighteenth century. Not only were there far fewer books to read, fewer topics and fewer distractions; the century enjoyed the advantages of a homogeneous—a real—culture. So Johnson could defer to the ultimate authority of the Common Reader. For the Common Reader represented, not the great heart of the people, but the competent, the cultivated, in general; and these represented the cultural tradition and the standards of taste it informed. And the competent, with their more-than-individual judgment, their better-than-individual taste, *were* common, for to be born into a homogeneous culture is to move among signals of limited variety, illustrating one predominant pervasive ethos, grammar and idiom (consider what the eighteenth century did with Homer) and to acquire discrimination as one moves. But to-day the more one is exposed to the circumambient confusion, the worse (apart from unusual luck in opportunity and training) is one's taste likely to be.

There is no Common Reader: the tradition is dead.[1] Its dissolution has caused no wide lament, having, in the nature of the case, for the most part escaped notice. Mr. H. G. Wells, attention having been called to it, would not be alone in feeling that we had not suffered any very great loss: Marxist communism is being much worn. Nevertheless, I am assuming for the moment that the reader of this pamphlet deplores the loss and agrees that it should be, if possible, repaired. The justification for the attitude will, perhaps, come out later.

It is plain, then, that if literary culture is to be saved it must be by conscious effort; by education carefully designed to meet the exigencies of the time—the lapse of tradition, the cultural chaos and the hostility of the environment. It would not be merely with the 'culture' of individuals that such an effort would be concerned— with adding to 'the few who can talk intelligently about Stendhal, Proust and Henry James' (though the more of them there are the better). Nevertheless an attempt like Mr. Pound's to 'give a man an orderly arrangement of his perceptions in the matter of taste' is immediately relevant: we are certainly concerned with the 'culture' of individuals, if with something more.

---

[1] [Any discrepancy there might appear to be between this pamphleteering emphasis and p. 16 above will hardly trouble the reader.]

EDUCATION AND THE UNIVERSITY

Mr. Pound dismisses with scornful, but not too scornful, unceremoniousness the academic handling of literary education. He sees that the kind of accumulation represented by university 'Arts' courses is not education at all, but rather disablement. Reform needs to be approached in a spirit the reverse of that which disinters 'forgotten poets of the eighteenth century.' And Mr. Pound is exhilaratingly drastic in his proposals for jettison and disencumbrance. If at the first turning over of the pages much that he says seems extravagant and perverse, one is prepared to consider it respectfully because of the promise of rare adequacy contained in his suggestions of principle. (For disencumbrance implies principles for positive ordering.)

Early in his essay he says:

> It appears to me quite tenable that the function of literature as a generated prize-worthy force is precisely that it does incite humanity to continue living; that it eases the mind of strain, and feeds it, I mean definitely as *nutrition of impulse*.

Again, having asked,

> Has literature a function in the State, in the aggregation of humans, in the republic, in the *res publica* . . .

he answers:

> It has. . . . It has to do with the clarity of 'any and every' thought and opinion. It has to do with maintaining the very cleanliness of the tools, the health of the very matter of thought itself. Save the rare and very limited instances of invention in the plastic arts, or in mathematics, the individual cannot think or communicate his thought, the governor and legislator cannot act effectively or frame his

108

laws, without words, and the solidity and validity of these words is in the care of the damned and despised *literati*. When their work goes rotten—by that I do not mean when they express indecorous thoughts—but when their very medium, the very essence of their work, the application of word to thing goes rotten, i.e. becomes slushy and inexact, or excessive or bloated, the whole machinery of social and of individual thought and order goes to pot.

A complete idea of literature may not be explicit here, but so unusual an adequacy is implied that, at first reading, one cannot believe that practical suggestions based on convincing, or at least persuasive, principles of selection and ordering will not follow. But this is the 'minimum basis for a sound and liberal education in letters' that Mr. Pound, summarizing his recommendations, finally prescribes:

MR. POUND'S PRESCRIPTION

CONFUCIUS.—'In full . . .'

HOMER.—'In full . . .'

OVID.—'And the Latin "personal" poets, Catullus and Propertius. . . .'

A PROVENÇAL SONG BOOK.—'With cross references to Minnesingers, and to Bion, perhaps thirty poems in all.'

DANTE.—'"And his circle" . . .'

VILLON.—

PARENTHETICALLY.—'Some other medieval matter might be added, and some general outline of history of thought through the Renaissance.'

VOLTAIRE.—'. . . some incursion into his critical writings . . . and some dip into his contemporaries (prose).'

STENDHAL.—'(At least a book and a half).'

FLAUBERT.—'(omitting *Salammbo* and the *Tentation*)—And the GONCOURTS.'

GAUTIER, CORBIÈRE, RIMBAUD.

EDUCATION AND THE UNIVERSITY

It may be thought that some injustice has been done to Mr. Pound in extracting this summary from the rest of the essay, and if nothing were said about the accompanying commentary and statement of principles there would be injustice. But, as examination of these principles will show, justice does not make Mr. Pound's prescription any more persuasive.

His great concern is, rightly, to save the student from the usual laborious dissipation, to put him in the way of the concentrated reading that will truly educate him by giving him, as it were, the essential structure of literary experience, the types and principles that will enable him to fend for himself, to organize, extend and consolidate. Literature is desolatingly vast. 'But,' says Mr. Pound, 'the books that a man needs to know in order to "get his bearings," in order to have a sound judgment of any bit of writing that may come before him, are very few.' This, in a sense, is true, and salutarily said. Yet more than Mr. Pound indicates here goes to 'sound judgment,' to education, to competence in literature. And if again it is suspected that the context makes the apparent inadequacy look different, it may be confidently replied that quotation in this case does no injustice.

What, then, to begin with, are the criteria by which Mr. Pound arrives at his 'minimum basis for a sound and liberal education in letters'?—'In introducing a person to literature,' he says, 'one would do well to have him examine works where language is efficiently used; to devise a system for getting directly and expeditiously at such works, despite the smoke-screens erected by half-knowing and half-thinking critics. . . . Great literature is simply language charged with meaning to the utmost possible degree.' The definition is not complete, but it

does at least suggest a very good corrective to the academic
—and general—habit of discussing literature in terms of
Hamlet's and Lamb's personalities, Milton's universe,
Johnson's conversation, Wordsworth's philosophy, and
Othello's or Shelley's private life; and the approach it
indicates promises to be correspondingly profitable. One
is certainly not prepared for the perversities that follow
when Mr. Pound comes to particular recommendations.
These are indeed perverse in that they belie the best
insight expressed in his statements of principle.

MR. POUND'S PERVERSITY

Perversity is established as the note of the essay long
before the reader arrives at the 'résumé of conclusions'
('the result of twenty-seven years' thought on the subject')
that has been quoted. In Mr. Pound's classification the
important writers for the student are (*a*) the *inventors*,
'discoverers of a particular process or of more than one
mode and process,' and (*b*) the *masters*, 'inventors who,
apart from their own inventions, are able to assimilate
and co-ordinate a large number of preceding inventions.'
—'The point is,' he says, 'that if a man knows the facts
about the first two categories, he can evaluate almost any
unfamiliar book at first sight. I mean, he can form a just
estimate of its worth and see how and where it belongs
in this schema.' How, then, we ask, does it come that
Mr. Pound's estimates are apt to be so perverse, for surely
it is extravagant perversity that, for instance, excludes
Shakespeare and Donne from these two 'categories,' that
includes Gautier and excludes Baudelaire? The faint
apology for a reason offered as an after-thought in Shakespeare's case is the reverse of mitigation: 'For the purposes of general education we could omit all study of
monistic totemism and voodoo for at least fifty years, and

study of Shakespeare for thirty, on the ground that acquaintance with these subjects is already very widely diffused and that one absorbs quite enough knowledge of them from boring circumjacent conversation.' As for Donne, the 'song books' are full of people like him, who 'add but some slight personal flavour, some minor variant of a mode, without affecting the main course of the story,' and 'choice among them is the matter of taste, for you prefer Wyatt to Donne, Donne to Herrick, Drummond of Hawthornden to Browne, in response to some purely personal sympathy. . . .'

The perversity here (as generally) is, of course, largely wilful, expressing partly exasperation, and partly, no doubt, a notion of tactics. The exasperation that lets itself go to these lengths one must deplore, and the notion of tactics was certainly mistaken that excluded from the study of the art of 'charging language with meaning to the utmost possible degree' the greatest master of that art known to us, together with the poet whose revived influence has been among the chief agents in producing a modern poetry answering to Mr. Pound's definition of great literature.

But we cannot really believe that he thought the significance of Shakespeare and of Donne so obvious that the denial would provoke the affirmation; whatever policy there may have been in his perversity, it was not this, for we cannot believe that he sees their full significance himself: his case is very interesting, and his pamphlet correspondingly profitable in other ways than he intended. He exhibits in himself with rare and illuminating conspicuousness certain deficiencies that are a large part of the futility that he deplores in academic literary education.

HOW TO TEACH READING

THE MISCONCEPTION OF TECHNIQUE

Some light is thrown on the staggering disparity between his generalities and his particular judgments by the following remark (he has just repeated that his subject is the 'art of getting meaning into words'): 'I am not talking about the books that have poured something into the general consciousness, but of books that show *how* the pouring is done or display the implements, newly discovered, by which one can pour.' The distinction is not altogether meaningless, but it will not bear the stress that Mr. Pound lays upon it, and the overstress betrays a serious deflection of interest in the critic. There is a great deal more need to assert that the pouring can *not* be studied apart from the thing poured. At any rate, the study of 'how the pouring is done' that does not find Shakespeare and Donne worth attention must be pronounced to have lost itself in the common and disastrous misconception of 'technique.'

The misconception illustrates the dangers attending those processes of abstraction which are inevitable in all criticism. We have to speak of 'technique' as something distinct from 'sensibility,' but technique can be studied and judged only in terms of the sensibility it expresses. The 'technique' that is not studied as the expression of a given particular sensibility is an unprofitable abstraction, remote from any useful purpose of criticism. A poet and a critic of Mr. Pound's achievement cannot be unacquainted with this truth, but he has lost it in the processes of critical analysis. Criticism involves analysis and abstraction, but the critic must see that his analysis is subtle enough, that his abstractions are the right ones, and that he does not, forgetting what they are, give them a status to which they have no right. Mr. Pound, like so many critics, better and worse, has not been vigilant enough.

EDUCATION AND THE UNIVERSITY

AN AMATEUR OF ABSTRACTIONS

He is, unhappily, an amateur of abstractions, and plumes himself on the general application and validity of certain of his analytic findings. In *How to Read* he distinguishes between three 'kinds of poetry' or 'manners' in which the 'language is charged or energized':

> *Melopœia*, wherein the words are charged, over and above their plain meaning, with some musical property, which directs the bearing or trend of the meaning.
> *Phanopœia*, which is a casting of images upon the visual imagination.
> *Logopœia*, 'the dance of the intellect among words,' that is to say, it employs words not only for their direct meaning, but it takes count in a special way of habits of usage, of the context we *expect* to find with the word, its usual concomitants, of its known acceptances, and of ironical play. It holds the aesthetic content which is peculiarly the domain of verbal manifestation, and cannot possibly be contained in plastic or in music.

This set of distinctions Mr. Pound uses as a main instrument of selection in arriving at his 'minimum basis for a sound and liberal education in letters.' But the abstractions, Melopœia, Phanopœia and Logopœia derive from an analysis so inadequate that there is hardly any purpose at all that one can think of them as serving. To begin with, none of them is equal to the status, as of co-operating entities, that Mr. Pound assigns them—and the naïvety of this assignment is not exaggerated here: 'All writing is built up of these three elements, plus "architectonics" or "the form of the whole," and to know anything about the relative efficiency of various works one must have some knowledge of the maximum already attained by various authors, irrespective of where and when.' It is hard to believe that Mr. Pound is really as naïve as all this, but his essay has certainly the effect of preaching that

'Melopœia,' 'Phanopœia' and 'Logopœia' can, and should, be studied apart. Such a study would have little to do with poetry. 'Melopœia,' for instance, the effect of the words as sound, is quite inseparable from their meaning and from the imagery they convey; these determine the 'musical property' as much as this 'directs the bearing or trend' of the meaning. The 'musical property' by itself is an abstraction so remote from the concrete experience of poetry as to be useless and so attractive (see such manuals as Mr. Greening Lamborn's *Rudiments of Criticism*) as to be vicious.

IMAGERY AND MR. POUND'S ' VISUAL IMAGINATION '

And imagery, to shift the attack, gets ludicrously inadequate treatment under 'Phanopœia.' For Mr. Pound not only surrenders to irrelevant and usurping abstractions; his analysis does pitifully less than justice to the complexities and subtleties of the use of words in poetry, of language 'charged with meaning to the utmost possible degree.' He seems to think (it is not for nothing that he has been associated with 'Imagism') that imagery is adequately dealt with as 'a casting of images upon the visual imagination.' But imagery in poetry is not merely visual, still less a matter of seeing little pictures; it may correspond to all the senses that can be involved, and it may range from incipient suggestion so faint as not to be consciously registered to complete explicit realization. (And images of muscular effort, which are common and important, may very obviously have—as other kinds may too—decisive effects upon 'Melopœia.') To take a random instance, imagery is exhibited in the following passage from *Macbeth* :

—All our service
In every point twice done, and then done double,

Were poor and single business, to contend
Against those honours deep and broad, wherewith
Your majesty loads our house.

In 'contend,' it will be conceded, we feel an unusual
physical force, yet perhaps very few, when challenged,
could say offhand how this comes, in what way it is
related to the image implicit in 'deep and broad,' or
what this is. The image is that, felt rather than seen, of a
full-flowing and irresistible river, and Shakespeare clearly
arrived at it by, characteristically, seizing on and realizing
the conventional metaphor of the king's being the 'fount
of honour.' But he has controlled realization to the requisite degree of incipience, so that the image is not felt to
quarrel with the following one of 'loads.' And in this
marvellously sure and subtle control of realization Shakespeare's genius is manifested as much as in the vividness
of his most striking imagery.

TECHNIQUE AND TRANSLATION

All this is merely to suggest how disastrously short Mr.
Pound falls in his account of the ways of 'charging or
energizing' language. These are such that the study of
poetic technique must be at the same time a training of
the critical sensibility; the cultivation of analysis that is
not also a cultivation of the power of responding fully,
delicately and with discriminating accuracy to the subtle
and precise use of words is worthless. This would seem
to be obvious enough. Yet in how many languages
besides one's own can one hope to acquire even the begin-
nings of a critical sensibility? Mr. Pound seems to contemplate competence in at least French, Provençal, Italian,
Greek, Latin, and Chinese as well as English. And this
is no more surprising than his gesture of reassurance: 'If
a man have not time to learn different languages he can,

at least, and with very little delay, be told what the discoveries were.' This 'telling about discoveries' can clearly
have little to do with the training of a critic (that is, with
real literary education) as Mr. Pound goes on to admit:
'If he wish to be a good critic he will have to look for himself.' But he insists on exacting one's unkindest verdict.
He suggests later that 'the reader who has been appalled
by the preceding parts and said, "Oh, but I can't learn
all these languages," may in some measure be comforted'
—by translations. 'He can learn the art of writing precisely where so many great local lights have learnt it.∴. . .'
This certainly throws some light on Mr. Pound's own
apparent conviction of polyglot competence. If one can
believe that 'technique' can be translated there is no
reason why one shouldn't believe it possible to acquire a
critical sensibility in the poetry of half a dozen languages,
from Chinese to Anglo-Saxon. But the 'technique' that
can be translated is not the technique that the critic who
described great literature as 'language charged with meaning to the utmost possible degree,' and its function as
'nutrition of impulse,' should be mainly interested in.
Mr. Pound has not been true to his best insight. It is
plain that his advice, if followed, would produce not education but a more or less elegantly pedantic dilettantism
like that which has its monument in the *Cantos*—indeed,
in the general body of Mr. Pound's work, apart from that
great poem, *Hugh Selwyn Mauberley*. (This is not to deny
the limited technical interest of a great deal of it.)

WHAT A LITERATURE IS

It is not only an inadequate notion of technique, and a
failure to grasp its relation to sensibility, that is betrayed
by Mr. Pound's wide-ranging eclecticism; we are brought
back to consider the incompleteness of his definition of

literature: 'Great literature is simply language charged with meaning to the utmost possible degree.' What more is needed does not come; it is renounced, just as the valid part offered is withdrawn, in his jaunty obtuseness to the language difficulty. In failing to grasp properly the relation of literature to language he fails even to suggest its relation to cultural tradition. Literature for him is a matter mainly of individual works, Chinese, English, Provençal, Anglo-Saxon and so on, written by individual artists who invent—or borrow from other individual artists —devices, processes and modes of charging language with meaning. The nature and conditions of this 'meaning,' apart from the admirable but inadequate hints already noted, he does not discuss.

His account (which for its salutary vigour and directness deserves to become a *locus classicus*) of the function of literature in the State as having 'to do with maintaining the very cleanliness of the tools, the health of the very matter of thought itself' implies a great deal more that he appears not to perceive; it demands expansion and development. The literature that can perform this function cannot be understood merely in terms of odd individual works illustrating 'processes' and 'modes'; it involves a literary tradition. And a given literary tradition is not merely, as it were by geographical accidents of birth, associated with a given language: the relation may be suggested by saying that the two are *of* each other. Not only is language an apt analogy for literary tradition; one might say that such a tradition is largely a development of the language it belongs to if one did not want to say at the same time that the language is largely a product of the tradition. Perhaps the best analogy is that used by Mr. Eliot in *Tradition and the Individual Talent* when he speaks of the 'mind of Europe.' 'Mind' implies both consciousness and memory, and a literary tradition is both: it is the consciousness and memory of the people or the cultural tradition in which it has developed.

Literary tradition so conceived involves, clearly, a good deal more than a tradition of writing and of writers. What more, the present writer does not know how to indicate better for immediate purposes than by quoting what he has written elsewhere. 'To those who take a serious interest in literature it must often seem as if their interest were curiously irrelevant to the modern world; curiously, because a serious interest in literature starts from the present and assumes that literature matters, in the first place at any rate, as the consciousness of the age. If a literary tradition does not keep itself alive here, in the present, not merely in new creation, but as a pervasive influence upon feeling, thought and standards of living (it is time we challenged the economist's use of this phrase), then it must be pronounced to be dying or dead. Indeed, it seems hardly likely that, when this kind of influence becomes negligible, creation will long persist. In any case, a consciousness maintained by an insulated minority and without effect upon the powers that rule the world has lost its function.' [Here followed a rather naïve characterization of the 'existing state of affairs.']

How this state of affairs developed, this is not the place to discuss. The passage has been quoted in order to suggest what is lacking in Mr. Pound's preoccupation with letters, and to enforce two related points: that one cannot be seriously interested in literature and remain purely literary in interests, and that one cannot discuss satisfactorily the 'basis of a sound and liberal education in letters' as a matter merely of the 'culture' of individuals.

Part II : Positive Suggestions

SUPPOSING, then, a university did its best to provide such an education, what would the basis be?

THE TRAINING OF SENSIBILITY

Everything must start from the training of sensibility, together with the equipping of the student against the snares of 'technique.' Everything must start from and be associated with the training of sensibility. It should, by continual insistence and varied exercise in analysis, be enforced that literature is made of words, and that everything worth saying in criticism of verse and prose can be related to judgments concerning particular arrangements of words on the page. In the nature of the case it is not possible to be as tabularly pat in prescription as Mr. Pound; his own explicitness, it has been shown, is unprofitable or illusory. The technique of analysis each teacher will, for the most part, have to develop for himself.[1] . . .

CRITICAL METHOD

It is hardly possible to insist too much on the training of sensibility as prior and irremissible. Literary study unassociated with it becomes, infallibly, 'academic' and barren —a matter of profitless memorizing, of practice in graceful or scholarly irrelevance, of scanning metrical feet and drawing graphs of plots and actions, or of 'discipline' at the higher navvying. Literary study, of course, cannot stop at the analysis of verse- and prose-texture. How to

[1 Instead of the paragraph of references and suggestions that followed in the original pamphlet I refer the reader back to pp. 69-84 above.]

go beyond and, without forgetting that everything done by the artist and experienced by the reader is done and experienced here, here and here at an advancing point in a sequence of words, deal with all that a critic has to deal with, the student must learn by frequenting a variety of examples of good criticism—examples illustrating, in different ways, criticism as a discipline both sensitive and strict of intelligence and sensibility. The best essays in T. S. Eliot's *Selected Essays* form an incomparable body of such examples. Here and there the hint for the development of more embracing critical thought out of local analysis ('practical criticism') is given with beautifully useful directness. Let the student consider, for instance, how Mr. Eliot in the essay·on Massinger, starting with comparisons between passages of Massinger's and Shakespeare's verse, arrives at comparative judgments concerning two ages.[1] He will then, at any rate, understand the injunction to attach, as far as possible, all that he wants to say about a given work to observations concerning technique, and will be safe from the kinds of interest in 'technique' that produced Mr. Pound's 'Melopœia,' 'Phanopœia,' 'Logopœia,' and the vowel-and-consonant analysis of the school manuals.

THE APPROACH TO SHAKESPEARE

But perhaps suggestions of a more particular and practical kind will be expected as to the advance from the criticism of, say, lyrical poems to more ambitious work. There is, clearly, no room for much detailed illustration here; a hint or two must suffice. At an early stage, then, the attempt should be made to apply seriously the axiom that poetry is made of words to the reading of Shakespeare. Suppose *Macbeth* to be the play. The *Arden*

[1 See Note at the end of this Appendix (p. 139).]

edition is useful because of the notes, many of which have the kind of value represented by this, which is the first:

> SCENE I. *Enter three Witches.* This scene is probably spurious. No dramatic interest or object is gained by its introduction.

When the good reasons, if any, for doubting that Shakespeare wrote the scene have been examined, that offered in the note may be made an opportunity for dealing with the common false approach to Shakespeare. For clearly the argument 'no dramatic interest or object is gained' is an appeal to a conception of 'drama': *Macbeth* is a drama, and a drama is a matter of characters in action and interaction, developing or revealing a scheme or plot; items in the play that develop the scheme, or forward the plot, are justified as serving a dramatic object; the others must be apologized for or explained away.

The student, probably, will not be at once struck by the mischievousness of these assumptions, for they are exemplified by all that he has read or heard as 'Shakespeare criticism.' Nor will he see at once anything wrong about the accompanying assumption, when it is pointed out: the assumption that every speech in the play is to be explained as throwing light on the character, 'psychology' or intentions of the speaker. The deviations and absurdities that this assumption leads to can be readily illustrated, and to do so is probably the best way of bringing home that one's caveat against the habit of regarding Shakespeare as a great 'creator of characters' is not a mere pedantic whim. One turns up, say, Act I, Scene VI of *Macbeth*—the scene under the battlements at Dunsinane:

> *Duncan.* This castle hath a pleasant seat; the air
> Nimbly and sweetly recommends itself
> Unto our gentle senses.

Banquo.   This guest of summer,
    The temple-haunting martlet, does approve,
    By his lov'd mansionry, that the heaven's breath
    Smells wooingly here: no jutty, frieze,
    Buttress, nor coign of vantage, but this bird
    Hath made his pendent bed, and procreant cradle:
    Where they most breed and haunt, I have ob-
        serv'd,
    The air is delicate.

Here is a good instance of Shakespeare's marvellous power of using words to compel on the reader or listener a precise complex response, to evoke the combination of emotions and associations appropriate to the context ('appropriate,' clearly, calls for analysis). We note the insistence, throughout the passage, of the element represented by 'pleasant,' 'sweetly,' 'gentle'; it is so insistent that it appears even in a place so apparently inappropriate (on editorial inspection) as to elicit from the *Arden* editor the comment: 'probably a proleptic construction.' But

the air
Nimbly and sweetly recommends itself,

and the set of associations represented by 'nimbly' is equally important on the whole : we are in hill air, which is not only sweet, but fresh and vital—a sharp contrast to the smothering sense, already evoked, of the 'blanket of the dark.' But that is not all; every word in the passage contributes. Why, for instance, 'temple-haunting'? It co-operates with 'guest' and 'heaven' to evoke the associations belonging to the 'sanctity of hospitality': for 'heaven,' reinforced by 'temple,' is not merely the sky where the fresh winds blow. Nevertheless the suggestion of altitude is potent:

no jutty, frieze,
Buttress, nor coign of vantage, . . .

—'above the smoke and stir of this dim spot.' But why 'martlet'? The bird, with its swift vitality and exquisite frail delicacy, represents a combination analogous to 'nimbly and sweetly.' But more; its 'pendent bed,' secure above the dizzy drop, is its 'procreant cradle'; and 'procreant' is enforced by 'breeds': all these suggestions, uniting again with those of 'temple' and 'heaven,' evoke the contrast to 'foul murder'—life springing swift, keen and vulnerable from the hallowed source.

There is no need to enlarge upon the dramatic potency of the effect thus roughly analysed. And yet it is to a great extent independent of the speakers (though, of course, Banquo and Duncan bring in an intensifying irony). At any rate, it will be granted that an attention directed upon 'character' and 'psychology' is not favourably disposed for doing justice to the kind of thing Shakespeare does here with words.

He is doing this kind of thing everywhere. For Shakespeare's blank verse is a convention (so subtle that we forget it to be one) that enables him to play upon us, not merely through our sense of the character speaking, but also, and at the same time, directly; and the question, how much of the one and how much of the other it may be in any particular case, does not arise. Nor should, for the critic, the question: 'How does Macbeth come to have this marvellous poetic imagination, this gift of utterance?' (see Bradley [1]). But there is no need here to give further instances of the absurdities criticism is betrayed into by the approach through 'character.'

After some such start as this the possibilities of profitable Shakespeare study open inexhaustibly.[2] The analysis of

[1 I recommended at this point Miss M. C. Bradbrook's *Elizabethan Stage Conditions*, which, unhappily, has now been out of print for years.]

[2 For illustration of ' how analysis may proceed to the wider relations of symbolism and so on ' I recommended L. C. Knights' verse and imagery may be related to more embracing criticism in such an exercise as the comparison (how unhappily 'stock'!) of *Antony and Cleopatra* with *All for Love*. It will be found that the essential points of difference between the two works as plays and poems can be arrived at by a developing criticism that starts with the verse, the characteristics of the two poets in imagery and rhythm and so on, and, in general, the ways in which they use the English language.

THE PROBLEM OF PROSE

These are the merest hints, but (with the references to the various critics) they should be enough. It will be noted that all the exemplifying has been from poetry. Prose demands the same approach, but admits it far less readily—it is not for nothing that criticism of the novel has hardly yet begun. With the novel it is so much harder to apply in a critical method the realization that everything that the novelist does is done with words, here, here and here, and that he is to be judged an artist (if he is one) for the same kind of reason as a poet is. Poetry works by concentration; for the most part, success or failure is obvious locally, in such passages as can be isolated for inspection. But prose depends ordinarily on cumulative

How Many Children Had Lady Macbeth?, which may still be had of Heffer, Cambridge.] It is the *start* that is illustrated above, the examination of what Shakespeare does locally with words. Such examination would be furthered by comparisons between characteristic passages of Shakespeare and of Gerard Manley Hopkins (hints are thrown out in the chapter on Hopkins in the present writer's *New Bearings in English Poetry*). [There is now D. A. Traversi's *Approach to Shakespeare* (Sands). This seems to me by far the best introduction and aid to the critical study of Shakespeare. Its compression, its intelligence, and its very questionableness (the way in which it provokes questions and, sometimes, disagreements) makes it an ideal book to start discussion groups with. I have used it very successfully in this way with First Year undergraduates.]

effect, in such a way that a page of a novel that is as a whole significant may appear undistinguished or even poor (consider, for instance, Hardy [1]: Virginia Woolf, on the other hand, like certain other moderns, stakes all on local success). Yet though the devising and applying of a critical technique may be found difficult in the case of prose-literature it should not, with the aids already cited (to which *The Problem of Style*,[2] by J. Middleton Murry, and *Fiction and the Reading Public*,[3] by Q. D. Leavis, may be added), be impossible. Out of a School of English that provided the training suggested here might come, not only a real literary criticism of Shakespeare, but a beginning in the criticism of the novel.

EQUIPMENT FOR SELF-DIRECTION

It should not have been gathered that no other kind of attention to Shakespeare is contemplated besides the critical work exemplified, or that the student is to be concerned merely with isolated texts. The aim here is to insist on the essentials, the equipment and the training that will enable the student to look after himself. Having learnt to read critically he will not be in danger of the laborious and stupefying dissipation that usually passes for study. He will, too, have been effectively trained against

[1] I am afraid I have given up my long endeavour to see Hardy as a great novelist.]

[2] Critical reading of any one of these books will be helped by the others.

[3] This book, though not primarily concerned with the literary criticism of the novel, contains much valuable suggestion for the critical technique desiderated.

[I leave those light-hearted sentences about the 'criticism of the novel' as they stood. Actually, nothing helpful in respect of that problem can be said briefly. I hope to bring out before long in collaboration with Q. D. Leavis a book that deals with the grounds and methods of the critical study of novels.]

the reverent approach to the 'masters' that so generally precludes contact with them, though in cases where there is a particularly powerful and misleading consensus of conventional valuation he might be put on the alert. For instance, where the lesser Elizabethan dramatists are concerned, he might be asked whether even Mr. Eliot, good as his commentary is, has done much to undo the bad work of Lamb and Swinburne.

THE IDEA OF TRADITION

Literary history and knowledge of the background, social and intellectual, remain, of course, indispensable. They should, and associated with this critical training they can, be made to serve an essential end: the understanding, so lamentably absent in Mr. Pound, of what a literature is and what a tradition.

The relation of the individual artist to others, to the contemporary world and to the past, to be grasped at all, must be grasped in some limited particular instances. Again the advantage that Mr. Pound's inadequacies give him in exposition comes out, for it is difficult here to illustrate both briefly and convincingly; and yet the attempt must be made. For illustration there is good reason (to be mentioned later) for choosing one instance, or set of instances, in especial—one of which Mr. T. S. Eliot has facilitated the study. Here, then, in earnest of practical responsibility (to be skipped by those who dislike the pedagogic and obvious), is a

SCHEME OF WORK

Ponder the first three essays in Section V of T. S. Eliot's *Selected Essays* ('The Metaphysical Poets,' 'Andrew Marvell,' 'John Dryden'). Read the Introduction to Professor

EDUCATION AND THE UNIVERSITY

Grierson's *Metaphysical Lyrics and Poems of the Seventeenth Century*, paying special attention to the paragraph on p. xv that describes the characteristics of the Metaphysicals:

> . . . the more intellectual, less verbal, character of their wit compared with the conceits of the Elizabethans; the finer psychology of which their conceits are often the expression; their learned imagery; the argumentative, subtle evolution of their lyrics; above all, the peculiar blend of passion and thought, feeling and ratiocination which is their greatest achievement. . . .

Test this account by analysis (using the technique developed in the training suggested above) of various poems of Donne in comparison with poems of Campion: the analysis will be found to be in great measure an illustration and expansion of Professor Grierson's account. Explore Mr. Eliot's suggestion (in the essay on 'The Metaphysical Poets'[1]) of affinities between this verse and Shakespeare's (sonnets as well as blank verse), Middleton's (see the essay on him), Tourneur's (see the essay on Massinger) and Chapman's. Contrasts with Milton (his blank verse primarily, but comparison between his *Avenge, O Lord*, and Donne's *At the round earth's imagin'd corners, blow*, is also illuminating) will help to make the case plain. At this point should be broached the question of the varying relation between English poetry and the spoken language,[2] and of the tendency (why as a rule deplorable?) to the formation of specifically 'poetic' styles. Examine in analysis of particular poems in Grierson the likenesses and differences between Donne and the later Metaphysicals: Herbert (see pp. 231-233 of W. Empson's

[1 For an extremely valuable discussion of those Metaphysicals who are to be distinguished from among the group as being 'metaphysical' in the strict sense of the adjective, the student should go to James Smith's essay on 'Metaphysical Poetry' in *Determinations* (edited by F. R. Leavis).]

[2 See Chapter I of my *Revaluation*.]

Seven Types of Ambiguity),[1] Vaughan, King, Marvell, Cowley and others. Do comparisons between representative poems of the seventeenth and nineteenth centuries, in order to bring out the advantage the seventeenth-century poets enjoyed in being in the 'tradition of wit' (type-comparison: Herbert's *Love* with No. 711 in the old *Oxford Book of English Verse*). Illustrate, again by analytic examination of particular poems, Professor Grierson's account (Introduction, p. li) of the transition to Dryden [2]:

> . . . His development was on the line of Donne and the Metaphysicals, their assimilation of poetic idiom and rhythm to that of the spoken language, but the talk of which Dryden's poetry is an idealization is more choice and select, less natural and fanciful, and rises more frequently to the level of oratory.

And pursue the line to its end in Pope as Professor Grierson suggests (p. lvii):

> . . . But wit which is not passionate and imaginative must appeal in some other way, and in Dryden it began to do so by growing eloquent. The interest shifted from thought to form, the expression not the novelty of the thought, wit polished and refined as an instrument of satire and compliment and declamation on themes of common interest. Dryden and Pope brought our witty poetry to a brilliant close.

The predominance, in various forms, of Milton from Thomson through Gray, Cowper and Akenside to Wordsworth, and, allied with Spenser, through Keats to Tennyson, though demanding separate study, must receive enough attention in this scheme of work to bring out the significance of what we have witnessed in

[1 For a *caveat* in regard to Empson, see p. 71, above.]
[2 On whom I recommended Mark van Doren's *John Dryden*, which is a valuable introduction to the Restoration background.]

our time: the reconstitution of the English poetic tradition by the re-opening of communications with the seventeenth century of Shakespeare, Donne, Middleton, Tourneur and so on. (This is the attack on the tradition of English poetry lamented by the higher reviewers, when they notice it [1]; it is discussed by the present writer in *New Bearings in English Poetry*.) What is meant by this 'reconstitution' should be examined in the poetry of Mr. Eliot, Mr. Pound's *Hugh Selwyn Mauberley*, and such other modern verse as seems to merit attention (opportunity for first-hand criticism).

THE LITERATURE OF THE PRESENT

The reason for the choice of this particular illustration of tradition will by now be plain: its focus of interest is in the present. To initiate into the idea of living tradition except in relation to the present is hardly possible. An addiction to literature that does not go with an interest in the literature of to-day, and some measure of intelligence about it, goes with the academic idea of tradition—traditionalism, that is, in the bad sense. And a lack of interest in the present means usually an incapacity for any real interest—the kind of interest that understands the meaning of 'technique'—in literature at all. Instead, we have the vested interest, for which Scott, Milton, Shelley, Donne and the rest are facts and fixed values (the fixture constituting 'tradition')—and confusion to him who threatens the stability or free circulation of the currency (there are no contemporary facts)! It is impossible, then, to believe in the 'Arts' course that doesn't encourage interest in the present; that is the test (interchangeable with the attitude in the matter of sensi-

[1 A ' period ' touch which I leave as a reminder of the general change in taste that has taken place in the last fifteen years.]

bility—is the priority of critical training recognized or not?). 'The important critic,' wrote Mr. Eliot, 'is the person who is absorbed in the present problems of art, and who wishes to bring the forces of the past to bear upon the solution of these problems.' Those concerned either with acquiring or imparting a 'minimum basis for a sound and liberal education in letters' would do well to ponder this sentence, for it has implications for them as well as for the critic—or, rather, critics is what they should be concerned to produce.

NOT A 'COURSE OF READING'

Literary history pursued in this spirit will be very different from the usual accumulation of dead and deadening knowledge about authors and periods. In the exemplifying there has obviously been no pretence of comprehensiveness or exhaustiveness. To recommend close analytic study of a few poems of each of the authors in question is not to discourage further attention to those authors, or attention to other authors. On the contrary, it is impossible that anyone who had done such close work locally would not in any case go on to further exploration, just as it is impossible that without such work the most voluminous reading should yield much profit. For further particularity of illustration (to take as a 'course of reading' what has been offered above would be to miss the point) there is no room and hardly more need. Armed in the ways suggested with a technique of reading, a trained sense for the significant, and types and analogues for dealing with further experience, the student may be left to educate himself (otherwise he is ineducable). He who has told himself with some precision just in what way *The Lotus-Eaters* and *Ulysses* are good, relating them through Keats back to Milton and Spenser, will not

EDUCATION AND THE UNIVERSITY

(unless examiners insist) find it necessary to check in detail Bradley's *Commentary* on *In Memoriam*, or (in any case) to read with intensive scrutiny any large proportion of Victorian verse. He who has intelligently compared Marvell's *Coy Mistress* with Morris's *Nymph's Song to Hylas* (*Oxford Book*, No. 802—809 in the new edition) will not go on to draw an extended parallel between Donne and Browning as metaphysical poets or to spend much time weighing the intellectual pretensions of Meredith.

THE CRITICAL APPROACH TO CRITICISM

It might be added that he who can discuss intelligently the relation between Eliot's criticism [1] and his creative achievement will not imagine that, whatever he is doing in reading Longinus, he is improving his critical armoury. Perhaps it should have been said explicitly at an earlier stage that the student needs equipping with a critique of criticism, for his prosperous development depends largely upon his ability to profit by critical aid. And when, in addition to having the critical equipment indicated earlier in this pamphlet, he has cleared his mind about such groups of central issues as 'Art and Morality [2] and 'Impersonality,' [3] and formed an idea of what really saying any-

[1 I had here a reference to Coleridge, but have come to see that he doesn't at all serve the purpose I have in mind. *Biographia Literaria* is the work of a genius, but it won't yield much profit to any but an experienced and well-equipped critic.]

[2 Chapters VIII, IX and X of I. A. Richards's *Principles of Literary Criticism* are useful at the commonsense level, if the quasi-scientific suggestion is discounted. Certain obviously relevant essays and notes of D. H. Lawrence's reprinted in *Phoenix* are worth looking up.]

[3 The central theoretical texts, of course, are in T. S. Eliot, notably in ' Tradition and the Individual Talent ' and ' The Function of Criticism.' Pages 249-253 of I. A. Richards's *Principles* will be found helpfully suggestive—if, again, the scientific psychology is discounted ; and if the helpless attitude about the possibilities of

thing about a work of art is like, he will soon discover how
little further critical aid to expect. The sooner he dis-
covers this the better, for to suppose that one ought to be
getting what actually isn't there to get is not only depressing but debilitating. He may even find something in
Aristotle if he knows that, so far from there being a critical
apparatus to be derived from the *Poetics*, he must take a
critical apparatus there. This is not to dispute that Aristotle was a great man or that the *Poetics* has great historical importance; but the *Poetics* does not, as the best of
the aids recommended certainly do, in itself provide the
means of making one a better critic. He who is clear
about these distinctions may frequent Coleridge, Arnold
and Johnson with profit. He will even, knowing that,
whatever the appearances, there is no criticism there,
have uses for 'Surveys' of English Literature. But he
will have no use at all for Hazlitt or Lamb. (Whoever,
for reading them, found himself clearer about any of their
subjects?)

OTHER LITERATURES

Having trained one's sensibility and grasped firmly the
significance of 'tradition' and 'a literature' in the literature of one's own language, one is equipped to profit by
incursions into other literatures. In French one might
reasonably aspire not merely to know the most important
writers—Villon, Racine, Molière, Stendhal, Flaubert,
Baudelaire, and so on—but to have some sense of French
literature as a whole. The relations with English will
inevitably affect the distribution of attention, one opening

analysis is dismissed. The theoretical approach, where this issue is
concerned, peculiarly needs to be associated with an approach by
'practical criticism.' But no theoretical discussion should be
allowed to go on for long at any distance from critical practice.]

for associated and associating studies being given by the line of Mr. Eliot's descent not yet mentioned, that coming from Baudelaire through Tristan Corbière and Jules Laforgue. It is characteristic of Mr. Pound's perversity to omit Baudelaire, and, while presenting Corbière, say nothing about his connexions.

One knows, of course, that much certainty of first-hand perception and judgment is impossible in a foreign language. But that knowledge has positive uses, and the sense of literary reality, the categories and the organization derived from experience make it possible to draw a larger profit than enters into Mr. Pound's scheme. One can read Dante, and helped, say, by Mr. Eliot's remarkable essay and by Mr. Santayana's *Three Philosophical Poets*, which Mr. Pound seems to despise, form something better than an academic notion of Dante's place in the European tradition. And so with the other significant things, major and minor: there is no need to specify further. The main point is that if one is uneducated in one's own literature one cannot hope to acquire education in any serious sense by dabbling in, or by assiduously frequenting, any other.

THE CLASSICS

Perhaps it is necessary to say explicitly that this holds also of the 'Classics,' from which, as we all know, our own literature derives. Interpret 'derivation' how we will, it gives no priority to Latin and Greek in education.[1] The common result of a classical training (need it be said that there are, of course, exceptions?) is to incapacitate from contact with literature for life. This is so because the

[1] Cf. the report of the Departmental Committee on *The Teaching of English in England* (H.M. Stationery Office, 1921).

'classic,' as Coleridge [1] noted (see *Biographia Literaria,*
C. 1), is trained to regard literature as a matter of mani-
pulating language according to rule and precedent—
language divorced from experience. The resulting 'taste,'
'judgment' and 'sense of fitness' (usually so strong in the
'classic') are almost insuperable bars to the development
of critical sensibility. For the 'classic,' Form is something
that Flecker, distinguished among modern poets, has and
Mr. Pound in *Hugh Selwyn Mauberley* most certainly hasn't.
Arrived at maturity, the 'classic' admires the prose of
C. E. Montague and the novels of Mr. Thornton Wilder
and Mr. Charles Morgan.[2] The moral is, not that the
Classics should be ejected from education, but that they
must be kept subsidiary to training in English.

THE 'MIND OF EUROPE'

The difference in spirit between the prescription offered
here and Mr. Pound's may be put, if not quite fairly, in
this way: the frequentation of other literatures here contemplated aims not at collecting a bag of tricks, but at
realizing an order. Mr. Pound's advice can lead at best

---

[1] And Wordsworth

' In fine,
I was a better judge of thoughts than words,
Misled in estimating words, not only
By common inexperience of youth,
But by the trade in classic niceties,
The dangerous craft of culling term and phrase
From languages that want the living voice
To carry meaning to the natural heart ;
To tell us what is passion, what is truth,
What reason, what simplicity and sense.'
THE PRELUDE, Bk. VI, 105-114.

[[2] There is no need to bring these two sentences up to date.
Flecker isn't altogether forgotten, so I haven't bothered to substitute
a reference to A. E. Housman (who is still a great poet). Mr. Morgan
still holds his place, and anyone can readily think of names to
substitute for the other two.]

to an elegant and scholarly eclecticism; the governing ideal here is to attain some sense of the 'mind of Europe,' that whole order referred to by Mr. Eliot, the order within which English literature has its place.

ANGLO-SAXON, ETC.

Inevitably, nothing like this education is possible where (as in most universities) the English course is 'English Language and Literature.' It should be plain that nothing is said here to discredit linguistic and philological studies as such. They, of course, like mathematics and physics, have their place, and, for those with the special capacity and vocation, their profit. But they have no profit for those for whom they are prescribed as essential to a humane education in letters. On the plea that unless he knows Anglo-Saxon and the History of the Language (most of which he will leave behind in the examination-room) he cannot properly understand modern English, the student is prevented from acquiring any real understanding of anything.[1] The means to a real understanding of modern English (such as constitutes an education) can be acquired only by a training of the kind sketched,

[1] The place of the study of Anglo-Saxon in relation to a humane education for the Englishman—i.e. as less irrelevant than the study of Persian or Sanskrit, but less relevant than the study of French, Italian, Latin, the non-literary arts, cultural history, psychology or some branches of anthropology—is authoritatively indicated by Professor and Mrs. Chadwick in the Preface to *The Growth of Literature* : ' One must admit that the amount of literature which is of independent native growth is much smaller in Anglo-Saxon than in Irish and Norse ; but it is of singular value and interest and by no means deserves the sad fate which has befallen it. We claim that more provision should be made for its study, *not as ancillary to a later literature which, owing to the break in continuity, can contribute nothing to its elucidation,* but for its own sake, and with the aid of other literatures, e.g., early Norse and Celtic, in a similar stage of growth.' The corollary of the passage italicized (for the purposes of the present argument) does not need stating explicitly.

and, for this, three years is short enough in any case. But no serious idea of education can have informed the spirit of these linguistic and philological compulsions. The following summary, drawn from a university handbook, is representative. The candidate, in his three years, must, in addition to his 'English' subjects, take either an Ancient Language, or French or German, or History. As 'English,' he must take Anglo-Saxon, Middle English, the History of the Language and Pre-Shakespearean Drama, and the kind of attention he has left for what we commonly mean by English literature (provided for in two or three more papers) may be imagined. That the History and Theory of Criticism and Practical Criticism are also examined in only emphasizes the point that what the student is made to suffer is not merely a deadening waste of time and energy, but exposure to a deadening and dehumanizing spirit. It does not need arguing that those who contrive and enforce such curricula do not know what they are educating for, or what education is. As sad confirmation, there is the further plea so commonly urged for these de-educating compulsions, that without them an English course provides no discipline. This, as things are, is commonly true, and where even the possibility of a profitable discipline is not perceived we may be sure that the start will not be easy. Meanwhile, as the corollary of discipline for discipline's sake, and equally hostile to education, we have, passing for an educated interest in literature, the elegant cult (with its token currency, and its specialized Good Form) of *belles lettres*.

'READING' IN SCHOOLS

With the universities ignoring their function, it would, of course, be idle to hope much of education in general. But what has been said has obvious applications at the school level, and much might be done if it were permitted, if there were teachers educated to do it, and if the examination system were not allowed to get in the way. Again the prior stress must fall on the training of sensibility, and this might profitably begin at an early age—but not with the help of the existing manuals of 'elementary criticism,' which are merely evidence of the general plight. Work at school could advance as far as the kind of critical reading of Shakespeare illustrated in this pamphlet. And, by a judicious use of literary history, education in what has been discussed as the 'idea of tradition' might be given a good start.

But a serious concern for education in reading cannot stop at reading. Practical criticism of literature must be associated with training in awareness of the environment [1] —advertising, the cinema, the press, architecture and so on, for, clearly, to the pervasive counter-influence of this environment the literary training of sensibility in school is an inadequate reply. Here is raised the whole question of the relation of reading to education and culture, a question which cannot be pursued now though it is one of the utmost importance, having obvious bearings on the question, discussed earlier, of the status and function of literature.

TRIBUTE AND VALEDICTION TO MR. POUND

Mr. Pound may be amused that his pamphlet should have provoked this descent into pedagogy. It came inevitably in a serious attempt to face the problems he raised. He may deny that he raised them, but that he did raise them is the reason for treating his pamphlet seriously, as that he did not know he had raised them is perhaps the radical criticism of Mr. Pound.

[1] How this may be done is suggested in *Culture and Environment : The Training of Critical Awareness*, by Denys Thompson and the present writer.

NOTE TO PAGE 121

IT is, as I say, a hint rather than a worked out demonstra-tion of critical method, but, for the man experienced in analytic 'practical criticism,' it is a very valuable hint. A hint of a like order is to be found in the remarks on Beaumont and Fletcher in the essay on Ben Jonson:

> For there is work contemporary with Jonson's which is super-ficial in a pejorative sense in which the word cannot be applied to Jonson—the work of Beaumont and Fletcher. If we look at the work of Jonson's great contemporaries, Shakespeare, and also Donne and Webster and Tourneur (and sometimes Middleton), have a depth, a third dimension, as Mr. Gregory Smith rightly calls it, which Jonson's work has not. Their words have often a network of tentacular roots reaching down to the deepest terrors and desires. Jonson's most certainly have not ; but in Beaumont and Fletcher we may think that at times we find it. Looking closer, we discover that the blossoms of Beaumont and Fletcher's imagination draw no sustenance from the soil, but are cut and slightly withered flowers stuck into sand.
>
> > Wilt thou, hereafter, when they talk of me,
> > As thou shalt hear nothing but infamy,
> > Remember some of these things ? . . .
> > I pray thee, do ; for thou shalt never see me so again.
> >
> > Hair woven in many a curious warp,
> > Able in endless error to enfold
> > The wandering soul ; . . .
>
> Detached from its context, this looks like the verse of the greater poets ; just as lines of Jonson, detached from their context, look like inflated or empty fustian. But the evocative quality of the verse of Beaumont and Fletcher depends upon a clever appeal to emotions and associations which they have not themselves grasped ; it is hollow. It is superficial with a vacuum behind it ; the superfices of Jonson is solid. It is what it is ; it does not pretend to be another thing.

The relation can be pointed out between this kind of criticism and the quality of intelligence exemplified very notably in (say) the general essay on the eighteenth century that appeared first as an introduction to the satires of Johnson. This essay, unhappily, is not contained in *Selected Essays*, but it is to be found in the 'World's Classics' volume called *English Critical Essays, XX Century*. It is a piece of writing of which, in its unmannered precision, its sure and sensitive economy, and the purity and adequacy of its concern to be transparent to the significant facts, seen in their significant relations, one can say to an undergraduate: 'You can't write like that, but it can do you nothing but good to try. If there is such a thing as a model of critical writing to point to, there you have it.'—

> It is as dangerous to generalize about the poetry of the eighteenth century as about that of any other age ; for it was, like any other age, an age of transition. We are accustomed to make a rough tripartite division between the poetry of the age of Pope, the poet of sentimental philosophizing—Thomson, Young, Cowper—and the early Romantic movement. What really happened is that after Pope there was no one who thought and felt nearly enough like Pope to be able to use his language quite successfully ; but a good many second-rate writers tried to write something like it, unaware of the fact that the change of sensibility demanded a change of idiom. Sensibility alters from generation to generation in everybody, whether we will or no ; but expression is only altered by a man of genius. A great many second-rate poets, in fact, are second rate just for this reason, that they have not the sensitiveness and consciousness to perceive that they feel differently from the preceding generation, and therefore must use words differently. In the eighteenth century there are a good many second-rate poets : and mostly they are second-rate because they were incompetent to find a style of writing for themselves, suited to the matter they wanted to talk about and the way in which they apprehended this matter.

The quiet precision, economy and lucidity of that, free as it is from all technicality or quasi-technicality, could have come only from an intelligence that is at the same time a trained critical sensibility: a vast amount of particular perception and critical analysis is implicitly there.

Perhaps as illustrative exercises in critical method—attempts to conduct a critical argument in terms constantly related as closely as possible to judgments about particular places in particular texts—I may refer to certain things of my own: the chapters on Shelley and Keats in *Revaluation*, and the essay on 'The Irony of Swift' in *Determinations*.

APPENDIX III

MASS CIVILIZATION AND
MINORITY CULTURE*

* Written in 1930, first published as a pamphlet
in that year, and reprinted here with only a minor
corrective touch.

And all wise and experienced persons know, that bad and mean writings, of particular tendencies, will secure tenfold the number of readers of good and high productions. Popular authors cannot bear to admit or hear this. But how can it be otherwise? Will the uncultivated mind admire what delights the cultivated? Will the rude and coarse enjoy what is refined? Do the low endure the reasonings which justify subordination? Will the butterflies of fashion encourage any marks of distinction but their own gay colours?

The Autobiography, Times, Opinions and
Contemporaries of Sir Egerton Brydges

All things are a flowing
Sage Heracleitus says;
But a tawdry cheapness
Shall outlast our days.

Even the Christian beauty
Defects—after Samothrace;
We see τὸ καλὸν
Decreed in the market place.

*   *   *   *   *

O bright Apollo
τίν ἀνδρα, τίν ἤρωα, τίνα θεὸν,
What god, man or hero
Shall I place a tin wreath upon!

Ezra Pound, *Hugh Selwyn Mauberley*

Appendix III

MASS CIVILIZATION AND MINORITY CULTURE

And this function is particularly important in our modern world, of which the whole civilization is, to a much greater degree than the civilization of Greece and Rome, mechanical and external, and tends constantly to become more so.

Culture and Anarchy, 1869

FOR Matthew Arnold it was in some ways less difficult. I am not thinking of the so much more desperate plight of culture to-day,[1] but (it is not, at bottom, an unrelated consideration) of the freedom with which he could use such phrases as 'the will of God' and 'our true selves.' To-day one must face problems of definition and formulation where Arnold could pass lightly on. When, for example, having started by saying that culture has always been in minority keeping, I am asked what I mean by 'culture,' I might (and do) refer the reader to *Culture and Anarchy*; but I know that something more is required.

In any period it is upon a very small minority that the discerning appreciation of art and literature depends: it is (apart from cases of the simple and familiar) only a few who are capable of unprompted, first-hand judgment. They are still a small minority, though a larger one, who are capable of endorsing such first-hand judgment by genuine personal response. The accepted valuations are a kind of paper currency based upon a very small proportion of gold. To the state of such a currency

[1] 'The word, again, which we children of God speak, the voice which most hits our collective thought, the newspaper with the largest circulation in England, nay with the largest circulation in the whole world, is the *Daily Telegraph*!'—*Culture and Anarchy*.
It is the *News of the World* that has the largest circulation to-day.

the possibilities of fine living at any time bear a close relation. There is no need to elaborate the metaphor: the nature of the relation is suggested well enough by this passage from Mr. I. A. Richards, which should by now be a *locus classicus*:

> But it is not true that criticism is a luxury trade. The rearguard of Society cannot be extricated until the vanguard has gone further. Goodwill and intelligence are still too little available. The critic, we have said, is as much concerned with the health of the mind as any doctor with the health of the body. To set up as a critic is to set up as a judge of values. . . . For the arts are inevitably and quite apart from any intentions of the artist an appraisal of existence. Matthew Arnold, when he said that poetry is a criticism of life, was saying something so obvious that it is constantly overlooked. The artist is concerned with the record and perpetuation of the experiences which seem to him most worth having. For reasons which we shall consider . . . he is also the man who is most likely to have experiences of value to record. He is the point at which the growth of the mind shows itself.[1]

This last sentence gives the hint for another metaphor. The minority capable not only of appreciating Dante, Shakespeare, Donne, Baudelaire, Conrad (to take major instances) but of recognizing their latest successors constitute the consciousness of the race (or of a branch of it) at a given time. For such capacity does not belong merely to an isolated aesthetic realm: it implies responsiveness to theory as well as to art, to science and philosophy in so far as these may affect the sense of the human situation and of the nature of life. Upon this minority depends our power of profiting by the finest human experience of the past; they keep alive the subtlest and most perishable parts of tradition. Upon them depend the implicit standards that order the finer living of an age, the sense that this is worth more than that, this rather

[1] *The Principles of Literary Criticism*, p. 61.

than that is the direction in which to go, that the centre [1] is here rather than there. In their keeping, to use a metaphor that is metonymy also and will bear a good deal of pondering, is the language, the changing idiom, upon which fine living depends, and without which distinction of spirit is thwarted and incoherent. By 'culture' I mean the use of such a language. I do not suppose myself to have produced a tight definition, but the account, I think, will be recognized as adequate by anyone who is likely to read this pamphlet.

It is a commonplace to-day that culture is at a crisis. It is a commonplace more widely accepted than understood: at any rate, realization of what the crisis portends does not seem to be common. I am, for instance, sometimes answered that it has all happened before, during the Alexandrian period, or under the Roman Empire. Even if this were true it would hardly be reassuring, and I note the contention mainly in order to record my suspicion that it comes from Spengler,[2] where, of course, authority may also be found for an attitude of proud philosophic indifference. For Spengler, the inexorable cycle moves once more to its inevitable end. But the common absence of concern for what is happening is not to be explained by erudition or philosophy. It is itself a symptom, and a phrase for it comes aptly to hand in Mr. H. G. Wells' new book, *The Autocracy of Mr. Parham*: 'Essentially it was a vast and increasing inattention.'

It seems, then, not unnecessary to restate the obvious. In support of the belief that the modern phase of human history is unprecedented it is enough to point to the

[1] ' . . . the mass of the public is without any suspicion that the value of these organs is relative to their being nearer a certain ideal centre of correct information, taste and intelligence, or farther away from it.'—*Culture and Anarchy*.

[2] A good account of some aspects of the modern phase may be found in *The Decline of the West*, Vol. II, Chapter IV.

machine. The machine, in the first place, has brought about change in habit and the circumstances of life at a rate for which we have no parallel. The effects of such change may be studied in *Middletown*, a remarkable work of anthropology, dealing (I am afraid it is not superfluous to say) with a typical community of the Middle West. There we see in detail how the automobile (to take one instance) has, in a few years, radically affected religion,[1] broken up the family, and revolutionized social custom. Change has been so catastrophic that the generations find it hard to adjust themselves to each other, and parents are helpless to deal with their children. It seems unlikely that the conditions of life can be transformed in this way without some injury to the standard of living (to wrest the phrase from the economist): improvisation can hardly replace the delicate traditional adjustments, the mature, inherited codes of habit and valuation, without severe loss, and loss that may be more than temporary. It is a breach in continuity that threatens: what has been inadvertently dropped may be irrecoverable or forgotten.

To this someone will reply that Middletown is America and not England. And it is true that in America change has been more rapid, and its effects have been intensified by the fusion of peoples. But the same processes are at work in England and the western world generally, and at an acceleration. It is a commonplace that we are being Americanized, but again a commonplace that seems, as a rule, to carry little understanding with it. Americanization is often spoken of as if it were something of which the United States are guilty. But it is something

---

[1] 'One gains a distinct impression that the religious basis of all education was more taken for granted if less talked about thirty-five years ago, when high school "chapel" was a religio-inspirational service with a "choir" instead of the "pep session" which it tends to become to-day.'—*Middletown*, by R. S. and H. M. Lynd, p. 204. This kind of change, of course, is not due to the automobile alone.

146

from which Lord Melchett, our 'British-speaking' [1] champion, will not save us even if he succeeds in rallying us to meet that American enterprise which he fears 'may cause us to lose a great structure of self-governing brotherhoods whose common existence is of infinite importance to the future continuance of the Anglo-Saxon race, and of the gravest import to the development of all that seems best in our modern civilization.' [2] For those who are most defiant of America do not propose to reverse the processes consequent upon the machine. We are to have greater efficiency, better salesmanship, and more mass-production and standardization. Now, if the worst effects of mass-production and standardization were represented by Woolworth's there would be no need to despair. But there are effects that touch the life of the community more seriously. When we consider, for instance, the processes of mass-production and standardization in the form represented by the Press, it becomes obviously of sinister significance that they should be accompanied by a process of levelling-down.

Of Lord Northcliffe, Mr. Hamilton Fyfe, his admiring biographer, tells us (*Northcliffe: an Intimate Biography*, p. 270):

> He knew what the mass of newspaper-readers wanted, and he gave it to them. He broke down the dignified idea that the conductors of newspapers should appeal to the intelligent few. He frankly appealed to the unintelligent many. Not in a cynical spirit, not with any feeling of contempt for their tastes; but because on the whole he had more sympathy with them than with the others, and because they were as the sands of the sea in numbers. He did not aim at making opinion less stable, emotion more superficial.

---

[1] 'That would be one of the greatest disasters of the British-peaking people, and one of the greatest disasters to civilization.' —Lord Melchett, *Industry and Politics*, p. 278.

[2] *Ibid.*, p. 281.

He did this, without knowing he did it, because it increased circulation.

Two pages later we are told:

> The Best People did read the *Daily Mail*. It was now seen in first-class railway compartments as much as in third-class. It had made its way from the kitchen and the butler's pantry of the big country house up to the hall table.

'Giving the public what it wants,' is, clearly, a modest way of putting it. Lord Northcliffe showed people what they wanted, and showed the Best People that they wanted the same as the rest. It is enough by way of commentary on the phrase to refer to the history of the newspaper press during the last half-century: a history of which the last notable event is the surrender of the *Daily Herald* to the operation of that 'psychological Gresham Law' which Mr. Norman Angell notes:

> . . . the operation of a psychological Gresham Law; just as in commerce debased coin, if there be enough of it, must drive out the sterling, so in the contest of motives, action which corresponds to the more primitive feelings and impulses, to first thoughts and established prejudices, can be stimulated by the modern newspaper far more easily than that prompted by rationalized second thought.[1]

> Let us face the truth [says Mr. Norman Angell further on]: the conditions of the modern Press cause the Bottomleys more and more and the Russells and Dickinsons less and less to form the national character. The forces under review are not merely concerned with the mechanical control of ideas. They transform the national temperament.[2]

---

[1] *The Press and the Organisation of Society*, p. 33.

[2] *Ibid.*, p. 43.

Vide also p. 35: 'When Swift wrote certain of his pamphlets, he presented a point of view contrary to the accepted one, and profoundly affected his country's opinion and policy. Yet at most he circulated a few thousand copies. One of the most important was printed at his own expense. Any printer in a back street could have

All this, again, is commonplace, but commonplace, again, on which it seems necessary to insist. For the same 'psychological Gresham Law' has a much wider application than the newspaper press. It applies even more disastrously to the films: more disastrously, because the films have a so much more potent influence.[1] They provide now the main form of recreation in the civilized world; and they involve surrender, under conditions of hypnotic receptivity, to the cheapest emotional appeals, appeals the more insidious because they are associated with a compellingly vivid illusion of actual life. It would be difficult to dispute that the result must be serious damage to the 'standard of living' (to use the phrase as before). All this seems so obvious that one is diffident about insisting on it. And yet people will reply by adducing the attempts that have been made to use the film as a serious medium of art. Just as, when broadcasting is in question, they will point out that they have heard good music broadcasted and intelligent lectures. The standardizing influence of broadcasting hardly admits

furnished all the material capital necessary for reaching effectively the whole reading public of the nation. To-day, for an unfamiliar opinion to gain headway against accepted opinion, the mere mechanical equipment of propaganda would be beyond the resources of any ordinary individual.'

[1] 'The motion picture, by virtue of its intrinsic nature, is a species of amusing and informational Esperanto, and, potentially at least, a species of aesthetic Esperanto of all the arts; if it may be classified as one, the motion picture has in it, perhaps more than any other, the resources of universality. . . . The motion picture tells its stories directly, simply, quickly and elementally, not in words but in pictorial pantomime. To see is not only to believe; it is also in a measure to understand. In theatrical drama, seeing is closely allied with hearing, and hearing, in turn, with mental effort. In the motion picture, seeing is all—or at least nine-tenths of all.'—*Encyclopædia Britannica*, 14th Ed.: 'Motion Pictures: A Universal Language.'

The *Encyclopædia Britannica*, fourteenth edition, is itself evidence of what is happening: 'humanized, modernized, pictorialized," as the editors announce.

of doubt, but since there is here no Hollywood engaged in purely commercial exploitation the levelling-down is not so obvious. But perhaps it will not be disputed that broadcasting, like the films, is in practice mainly a means of passive diversion, and that it tends to make active recreation, especially active use of the mind, more difficult.[1] And such agencies are only a beginning. The near future holds rapid developments in store.

Contemplating that deliberate exploitation of the cheap response which characterizes our civilization, we may say that a new factor in history is an unprecedented use of applied psychology. This might be thought to flatter Hollywood, but, even so, there can be no room for doubt when we consider advertising, and the progress it has made in two or three decades. (And 'advertising' may be taken to cover a great deal more than comes formally under that head.) 'It ought to be plain even to the inexperienced,' writes an authority, Mr. Gilbert Russell (in *Advertisement Writing*), 'that successful copywriting depends upon insight into people's minds: not into individual minds, mark, but into the way average people

[1] Mr. Edgar Rice Burroughs (creator of Tarzan), in a letter that I have been privileged to see, writes: 'It has been discovered through repeated experiments that pictures that require thought for appreciation have invariably been box-office failures. The general public does not wish to think. This fact, probably more than any other, accounts for the success of my stories, for without this specific idea in mind I have, nevertheless, endeavoured to make all of my descriptions so clear that each situation could be visualized readily by any reader precisely as I saw it. My reason for doing this was not based upon a low estimate of general intelligence, but upon the realization that in improbable situations, such as abound in my work, the greatest pains must be taken to make them appear plausible. I have evolved, therefore, a type of fiction that may be read with the minimum of mental effort.' The significance of this for my argument does not need comment. Mr. Burroughs adds that his books sell at over a million copies a year. There is not room here to make the comparisons suggested by such documents as the *Life of James Lackington* (1791).

think and act, and the way they react to suggestions of various kinds.' And again: 'Advertising is becoming increasingly exact every day. Where instinct used to be enough, it is being replaced by inquiry. Advertising men nowadays don't say, "The public will buy this article from such and such a motive": they employ what is called market research to find out the buying motives, as exactly as time and money and opportunity permit, from the public itself.'

So, as another authority, Mr. Harold Herd, Principal of the Regent Institute, says (*Bigger Results from Advertising*): 'Now that advertising is more and more recruiting the best brains of the country we may look forward to increasingly scientific direction of this great public force.'

Mr. Gilbert Russell, who includes in his list of books for 'A Copy Writer's Bookshelf' the works of Shakespeare, the Bible, *The Forsyte Saga*, *The Oxford Book of English Verse*, *Fiery Particles* by C. E. Montague, and Sir Arthur Quiller-Couch's *The Art of Writing*, tells us that:

> Competent copy cannot be written except by men who have read lovingly, who have a sense of the romance of words, and of the picturesque and the dramatic phrase; who have versatility enough and judgment enough to know how to write plainly and pungently, or with a certain affectation. Briefly, competent copy is a matter not only of literary skill of a rather high order, but also skill of a particular specialized kind.

The influence of such skill is to be seen in contemporary fiction. For if, as Mr. Thomas Russell (author of *What did you do in the Great War, daddy?*), tells us, 'English is the best language in the world for advertising,' advertising is doing a great deal for English. It is carrying on the work begun by Mr. Rudyard Kipling, and, where certain important parts of the vocabulary are concerned, making things more difficult for the fastidious. For what is taking place is not something that affects only the environment of culture, stops short, as it were, at the periphery. This should be obvious, but it does not appear to be so to many who would recognize the account I have given above as matter of commonplace. Even those who would agree that there has been an overthrow of standards, that authority has disappeared, and that the currency has been debased and inflated, do not often seem to realize what the catastrophe portends. My aim is to bring this home, if possible, by means of a little concrete evidence. I hope, at any rate, to avert the change of extravagant pessimism.

For consider, to begin with, Mr. Arnold Bennett. The history of how the author of *The Old Wives' Tale* has since used his creative talents I will not dwell upon further than to suggest that such a history would have been impossible in any other age. It is Mr. Arnold Bennett, the arbiter of taste, that I have chiefly in mind. In this capacity too he has a history. If one reads the articles which he contributed to the *New Age* twenty years ago (they are reprinted in *Books and Authors*) it is to break into admiring comment again and again. It is, for instance, impossible not to applaud when he is impudent about the Professors:

> I never heard him lecture, but I should imagine that he was an ideal University Extension lecturer. I do not mean this to be in the least complimentary to him as a critic. His book, *Illustrations of Tennyson*, was an entirely sterile exercise, proving on every page that the author had no real perceptions about literature. It simply made creative artists laugh. They knew. His more recent book on modern tendencies displayed in an acute degree the characteristic inability of the typical professor to toddle alone when released from the leading strings of tradition.
>
> I fear that most of our professors are in a similar fix. There is Professor George Saintsbury, a regular Albert Memorial of learning.

> It may not be generally known (and I do not state it as a truth) that Professor Raleigh is a distant connection of the celebrated family of Pains, pyrotechnicians.

Yes, it is impossible not to applaud. And yet there is something in the manner—well, twenty years later we find it more pronounced:

> Nevertheless, though performances of Greek plays usually send me to sleep—so far off and incredible is the motivation of them, I murmur about the original author on reading some of the dialogues of Plato: 'This fellow knew exactly how to do it.' And of Homer: 'This fellow knew the whole job.' And of Aristotle: 'This is the only fellow who ever really could do it.' And when I first set eyes on the Acropolis at Athens I said out loud—no mere murmuring: 'These fellows could do it.' (*Evening Standard*, Jan. 19th, 1928.)

When I try to comment on the manner of this I can only murmur: 'Matthew Arnold could have done it.' It is, of course, not merely manner: the Man from the North brought something more fundamental with him. There is an ominous note in the first passage I quoted: 'It simply made creative artists laugh. They know.' Mr. Bennett is a creative artist, and Mr. Bennett knows. And for some years now Mr. Bennett has been the most powerful maker of literary reputations in England. To compute how many bad books a year, on the average, Mr. Bennett has turned into literature would hardly be worth the labour. It is enough to instance some of his achievements and to quote some of his pontifical utterances from the *Evening Standard*. Here is the typical achievement:

> Mr. Arnold Bennett's reputation as a maker of 'best sellers' has been heightened by the addition of one more to the list of other people's books which the public has clamoured for on his word.

153

Last week *Vivandiere* meant nothing to most people, and the name of Miss Phoebe Fenwick Gaye conveyed no more.

Then Mr. Arnold Bennett, in his weekly article on books in the *Evening Standard,* mentioned that *Vivandiere* was this young woman's first novel, and that it was very good.

The demand for the book which has suddenly arisen has cleared the first edition right out of existence, and still the clamour goes on. Martin Secker, the publishers, told the *Evening Standard* of the sudden overwhelming demand which followed Mr. Arnold Bennett's praise.

A member of the firm said:

'The demand was so great that the first edition was completely sold out and we have had to get busy with a second edition, which will be ready tomorrow.'

Mr. Arnold Bennett made in this way *Jew Süss.* He also made, I understand, *The Bridge of San Luis Rey*; for, though he saw through the academic critics, he takes readily to Academy art. But his critical prowess is best exhibited by quotation from the *Evening Standard*:

Nov. 22nd, 1928.—'*The Golden Age* is a destructive masterpiece.'

Dec. 13th, 1928.—'Mr. Eliot is a fine poet—sometimes, if not in that celebrated piece of verse, *The Waste Land*, at the mention of which the very young bow the head in adoration.'

May 3rd, 1928.—'Mr. Stanley Baldwin made no mistake about Mary Webb.'

Jan. 3rd, 1929.—'The novel is making progress. It has been galvanized by the very important experiments of James Joyce, D. H. Lawrence, R. H. Mottram, and Aldous Huxley: all of whom have brought something new into it. The biggest of these is, or was, James Joyce ... R. H. Mottram is a genius. He writes like a genius,' etc.

Nov. 8th, 1928.—' ... In particular I have failed to perceive any genuine originality in the method of *Mrs. Dalloway*. If originality there is, it fails of its object of presenting a character, . . . Here is Mr. Muir discussing the modern novel, and he makes but passing reference to D. H. Lawrence, and no reference at all to R. H. Mottram, the two novelists who more than any other of their contemporaries, continually disclose genuine originality, the two real British geniuses of the new age!'

Jan. 24th, 1929.—'I have just read Edith Sitwell's new poem, *Gold Coast Customs*. In its intense individuality, its frightening freshness of vision, its verbal difficulties, it stands by itself.'

Mr. Bennett, we perceive, is a judge of poetry as well as of the novel: he can distinguish. He is adequate to the subtle complexities of Miss Sitwell, but he will stand no nonsense from Mr. Eliot. And he has no misconception about the kind of success that alone can justify a poet:

> These parasites on society cannot, or apparently will not, understand that the first duty of, for instance, a poet is not to write poetry, but to keep himself in decency, and his wife and children if he has them, to discharge his current obligations, and to provide for old age. (*Evening Standard*, June 9th, 1927.)

No, it was not merely a manner that Mr. Bennett brought with him from the Five Towns. And it is not merely expression that one finds so gross in his critical vocabulary: 'Value for money'; 'let there be no mistake about it, this is a big book'; 'a high class poet'; ' . . . I enjoyed reading *Creative Writing*. It is full of chunks of horse-sense about writing.' But Mr. Bennett is capable of modesty: it has occurred to him, for instance, to be modest about his qualifications for judging poetry. And his modesty is, if possible, even more damning than his assurance. He writes in *Journal, 1929*:

> I met a poet there; he was modest; he remarked in a somewhat sad tone that I rarely mentioned poetry in my articles on new books. I told him that I gave poetry a miss

for the good reason that I had no technical knowledge of prosody. (True, you can have a knowledge of prosody without having a feeling for poetry, but you cannot properly assess poetry without knowing a lot about prosody.)

Mr. Bennett will not understand what is meant by saying that this would-be confession is, instead, self-betrayal: so complete is his ignorance about poetry.

How is it that he can go on exposing himself in this way without becoming a by-word and a laughing-stock? (For the author of *The Old Wives' Tale* is a public figure, and differs in this from the minor pontiffs who compete with him in the Sunday papers and elsewhere.) It is that there is no longer an informed and cultivated public. If there is no public to break into a roar of laughter when Mr. Bennett tells us that R. H. Mottram, like James Joyce, is a genius, or that D. H. Lawrence and R. H. Mottram (poor Mr. Mottram!) are the two real British geniuses of the new age, how should there be a public to appreciate Mr. Bennett's modesty about poetry? (For fiction, as we all know, is read and enjoyed.) Why should Mr. Bennett's pontifications make a stir when Mr. J. C. Squire, specialist in poetry and 'himself a poet,' can, in prefacing one of the best-known anthologies of modern verse (*Selections from Modern Poets*), write:

> Should our age be remembered by posterity solely as an age during which fifty men had written lyrics of some durability for their truth and beauty, it would not be remembered with contempt. It is in that conviction that I have compiled this anthology;

and Mr. Harold Monro, even more a specialist in poetry and also 'himself a poet,' in the *Introduction* to *Twentieth Century Poetry*:

> Is it a great big period, or a minutely small? Reply who can? Somebody with whom I was talking cried: 'They are all only poetical persons—*not* poets. Who will

be reading them a century hence?' To which I answered:
'There are so many of them that, a century hence, they may
appear a kind of Composite Poet; there may be 500 excellent poems proceeding from 100 poets mostly not so great,
but well worth remembering a century hence.'

Such pronouncements could be made only in an age
in which there were no standards, no living tradition
of poetry spread abroad, and no discriminating public.
It is the plight of culture generally that is exemplified
here.[1] In the *Advertisement* to the first edition of *Lyrical
Ballads* I light on this:

> An accurate taste in poetry, as in all other arts, Sir
> Joshua Reynolds has observed, is an acquired talent, which
> can only be produced by severe thought, and a long con-
> tinued intercourse with the best models of composition.

When Wordsworth wrote that, severe thought and long-
continued intercourse with the best models were more
widely possible than now. What distractions have come
to beset the life of the mind since then! There seems
every reason to believe that the average cultivated person
of a century ago was a very much more competent reader
than his modern representative. Not only does the
modern dissipate himself upon so much more reading of
all kinds: the task of acquiring discrimination is much
more difficult. A reader who grew up with Wordsworth

---

[1] 'For there is no such gulf between poetry and life as over-literary
persons sometimes suppose. There is no gap between our everyday
emotional life and the material of poetry. The verbal expression
of this life, at its finest, is forced to use the technique of poetry; that
is the only essential difference. We cannot avoid the material of
poetry. If we do not live in consonance with good poetry, we must
live in consonance with bad poetry. And, in fact, the idle hours of
most lives are filled with reveries that are simply bad private poetry.
On the whole evidence, I do not see how we can avoid the conclusion that a general insensitivity to poetry does witness a low level
of general imaginative life.'—I. A. Richards, *Practical Criticism*, pp.
319–20.

moved among a limited set of signals (so to speak):
the variety was not overwhelming. So he was able to
acquire discrimination as he went along. But the modern
is exposed to a concourse of signals so bewildering in their
variety and number that, unless he is especially gifted or
especially favoured, he can hardly begin to discriminate.
Here we have the plight of culture in general. The land-
marks have shifted, multiplied and crowded upon one
another, the distinctions and dividing lines have blurred
away, the boundaries are gone, and the arts and literatures of different countries and periods have flowed
together, so that, if we revert to the metaphor of 'language' for culture, we may, to describe it, adapt the sentence
in which Mr. T. S. Eliot describes the intellectual situation: 'When there is so much to be known, when there
are so many fields of knowledge in which the same words
are used with different meanings, when every one knows
a little about a great many things, it becomes increasingly
difficult for anyone to know whether he knows what he is
talking about or not.'

We ought not, then, to be surprised that now, when a
strong current of criticism is needed as never before, there
should hardly be in England a cultivated public large
enough to support a serious critical organ. The *Criterion*
carries on almost alone. It is accused of being solemn,
and seems to owe its new-found security to a specific
ecclesiastical interest. For the short-lived *Calendar of
Modern Letters*, as intelligent and lively a review as ever
appeared in English, died for lack of support. Whatever
support the *Dial* may have enjoyed on this side the Atlantic, it now comes no longer, and only the *New Adelphi* is
left to carry on with the *Criterion*. There is, of course,
the *Times Literary Supplement*, but it would be a misnomer
to call it a critical organ. For the hope of intelligent
reviewing we are left (apart from the *Criterion* and the

New Adelphi) to the *Nation and Athenaeum* and the *New Statesman*, and they, of course, have no room for any but short articles.

The critically adult public, then, is very small indeed: they are a very small minority who are capable of fending for themselves amid the smother of new books. But there is a relatively large public that goes for guidance to the *Observer* and the *Sunday Times*, and a still larger one that goes to weeklies like *John o' London's* (which have surprising circulations) Now it would take greater enterprise and vigour than are common in these publics to make much use of the kind of help to be found in such quarters. The reader must have a great deal more done for him. Again we have to learn from America: the problem has been solved there by the Book of Month Club and similar organizations. The problem is now rapidly being solved here, where The Book Society has already been followed by The Book Guild.

> Out of the thousands of books published every year [writes Miss Ethel Mannin for the Book Guild]—there are between 12,000 and 14,000—how on earth is the ordinary person to sift the sheep from the goats? Distinguished critics attempt to guide the public, but they are often so hopelessly 'high brow' and 'precious,' and simply add to the general confusion and bewilderment.
>
> When the aims of The Book Guild were explained to me, therefore, it seemed too good to be true—an organization which would cater *for the ordinary intelligent reader*, not for the highbrows—an organization which would realize. that *a book can have a good story and a popular appeal and yet be good literature*—be good literature and yet be absorbingly interesting, of the kind you can't put down once you've started, an organization which would not recommend a book as a work of genius simply because it had been eulogized by some pedantic critic or other, but which would conscientiously sift really good stuff out of the mass of the affected and pretentious which is just as tiresome as the blatantly third rate.

There are so many really good books written nowadays that it is utterly impossible for the ordinary person to keep track of them all—even the critics don't succeed in doing so. The Book Guild by means of its Recommended List of Alternative Titles is able, as it were, to keep its finger on the pulse of the best of contemporary work, whilst at the same time providing something for everybody and that something the best of its kind—etc.

As for the method, we may turn to the official account of 'How the Book Society operates':

> Publishers throughout the country are submitting their most important works in advance of publication to the selection committees. From these the Committee select their 'books of the month,' and in addition compile a supplementary list of others they can thoroughly recommend.
> On the morning of publication every member of the Book Society receives a first edition of the book the committee have chosen. Enclosed in this book is a copy of the 'Book Society News' which contains reviews by members of the committee both of the selected book and of those on the supplementary list. If any members feel that the book chosen is not *their* book, they may return it within five days and will receive by return whatever book they select in exchange from the supplementary list.

Mr. Hugh Walpole, Miss Clemence Dane (author of *Tradition and Hugh Walpole*), Mrs. Sylvia Lynd, Mr. J. B. Priestley (who wrote of a book of Mr. Walpole's: '*Rogue Herries* is a grand tale, a real full-time man's job in fiction, and everybody should read it'), and the President of Magdalen College, Oxford, then, have, with their compeers of The Book Guild, taken into their keeping the future of English taste, and they will undoubtedly have a very great influence.[1] The average member of their

[1] A member is reported as writing: 'No man likes to be told what is good for him, it is an affront to his intelligence. Neither will he allow Mr. Walpole nor Mr. Priestley nor John Milton to tell him

flocks will probably get through a greater amount of respectable reading than before. But the most important way in which their influence will work is suggested by this passage from a book I have already referred to, *Advertisement Writing*, by Mr. Gilbert Russell:

Some years ago a manufacturer was making some hundred of different patterns of the same article. His factory was therefore constantly concerned with small runs, necessitating frequent setting-up of machines. This was expensive, and the manufacturing economies of large-scale production were out of reach. It was seen that if the number of patterns could be reduced from hundreds to scores, factory economies could be effected. This course was beset with difficulties, however. The retail trade was accustomed to order individual patterns to suit individual shopkeepers, and the travellers were afraid of losing orders if they told their shopkeeper friends that individual preferences and fads could no longer be provided for, and orders must be booked from a score of standard patterns. Nevertheless the manufacturer was determined. What he did was to reduce his hundreds of patterns to the score that were most often ordered. The whole of his marketing policy became one of concentrating selling effort upon this score of patterns. The thing had to be done gradually. But this was the settled purpose which he had in mind, and his advertising policy had to conform to his marketing policy. For instance, in catalogues to the retail trade nearly all the former hundred patterns were mentioned, and most of them illustrated as they had always been, but the score or so of patterns that he was concentrating upon were illustrated in *colour*. And, exactly as expected, the vast

---

what to read. But he is simply a fool if he is not impressed by their decisions in matters of literary taste. And that is where the Book Society comes in.'

'The speaker had evidently no notion that there was a scale of value for judgments on these topics, and that the judgments of the *Saturday Review* ranked high on this scale, and those of the *British Banner* low; the taste of the bathos implanted by nature in the literary judgments of man had never, in my friend's case, encountered any let or hindrance.'—*Culture and Anarchy.*

bulk of the orders came in for these. Similarly, advertisements emphasized the standard lines, the object of the advertising policy being to educate the public into demanding what the manufacturer wanted to sell, so that the retail trade should order what the public actually demanded. In time, of course, all the patterns were dropped except the standard ones.

This saves a great deal of comment. Standardization advances to fresh triumphs.

The Book Society has at its command the psychological resources of modern advertising:

> How often, sitting in some strange house, have your eyes wandered to the bookshelves in an effort to get some idea of the character of its owner? The books you read are often a guide to your character. The Book Society will help you to get those books you most want to have on your bookshelf.[1]

We are reminded of the way in which the compatriots of George F. Babbitt are persuaded to express their personalities in 'interior decoration.' There is, in fact, a strong American flavour about the 'literature' of both concerns. Both, for example, make great play with the American adjective 'worth-while': 'Build a worth-while library!'; 'a worth-while book': 'I believe that the Book Society will prove to many people that a few pounds spent on new books in the year is a happy and worthwhile experience' (Mr. Hugh Walpole). The significance of this use, of course, lies in the atmosphere of uplift and hearty mass sentiment that the word brings with it. An appreciative member writes: 'Finally, as a member of the Book Society, I am conscious of a pleasant feeling of comradeship, it is something of a great adventure, original, happily conceived, well carried out, with friendly methods of working.'—Innocent enough, in all conscience. But there is, belonging to the same vocabu-

[1] *The Books you Read.* Published by the Book Society.

lary as 'worth-while,' another word that the sovereign powers of both organizations use even more—'high-brow.' And the attitude behind the word 'high-brow' is exhibited with commendable guilelessness by Mr. George A. Birmingham (Canon Hannay) of The Book Guild. This reverend gentleman writes in *The Book Guild Bulletin* for July 14th, 1930:

> The detective novel writers have their own clientele, though they make no appeal to the young ladies who throng the counters of Boots' libraries and but little to the sheep-like crowd who follow the dictates of high-brow literary critics.

Lest the point should be missed he repeats it:

> . . . not food for the Messrs. Boots' young ladies or for the literary sheep whom I have already mentioned.

If the independent and intelligent critics who unpack the books chosen for them by Mr. George A. Birmingham, Miss Ethel Mannin,[1] Mr. Walpole, and Miss Clemence Dane [2] do not know now how they should feel towards the snobs who question the taste of these authorities—then they are not the independent and intelligent critics they are taken for.

'High-brow' is an ominous addition to the English language. I have said earlier that culture has always

---

[1] The *Nation and Athenaeum* reviewer of Miss Mannin's recent book, *Confessions and Impressions*, says: ' . . . I confess that the impression her book makes upon me is that it is cheap, crude, vulgar and uneducated.'—*Nation and Athenaeum*, August 9th, 1930.

[2] 'And it is easy to believe that the modern English novel, which is suffering so severely nowadays from specialists, high-brows, and cranks, will benefit as thoroughly from its course of Edgar Wallace and Sax Rohmer as it did a century ago from its dose of Monk Lewis, Maturin and Mrs. Radcliffe.'—*Tradition and Hugh Walpole*, by Clemence Dane, p. 27.

There is nothing more discussible than this in the windy, pretentious, eloquent vacuity of Miss Dane's book, which received respectful attention on the front page of the *Times Literary Supplement*, July 31st, 1930.

been in minority keeping. But the minority now is made conscious, not merely of an uncongenial, but of a hostile environment. 'Shakespeare,' I once heard Mr. Dover Wilson say, 'was not a high-brow.' True: there were no 'high-brows' in Shakespeare's time. It was possible for Shakespeare to write plays that were at once popular drama and poetry that could be appreciated only by an educated minority. *Hamlet* appealed at a number of levels of response, from the highest downwards. The same is true of *Paradise Lost, Clarissa, Tom Jones, Don Juan, The Return of the Native*. The same is not true, Mr. George A. Birmingham might point out, of *The Waste Land, Hugh Selwyn Mauberley, Ulysses* or *To the Lighthouse*. These works are read only by a very small specialized public and are beyond the reach of the vast majority of those who consider themselves educated. The age in which the finest creative talent tends to be employed in works of this kind is the age that has given currency to the term 'high-brow.' But it would be as true to say that the attitude implicit in 'high-brow' causes this use of talent as the converse. The minority is being cut off as never before from the powers that rule the world; and as Mr. George A. Birmingham and his friends succeed in refining and standardizing and conferring authority upon 'the taste of the bathos implanted by nature in the literary judgments of man' (to use Matthew Arnold's phrase), they will make it more and more inevitable that work expressing the finest consciousness of the age should be so specialized as to be accessible only to the minority.

'Civilization' and 'culture' are coming to be antithetical terms. It is not merely that the power and the sense of authority are now divorced from culture, but that some of the most disinterested solicitude for civilization is apt to be, consciously or unconsciously, inimical to culture. Mr. H. G. Wells, for example, belongs, for the minority, to the past, but it is probable that he represents a good deal of the future. And he returns the compliment paid him by the minority. In his last book, *The Autocracy of Mr. Parham*, he makes his butt, a wax-work grotesque labelled 'Oxford Don,' representative not only of tribal nationalism, imperialism, and The Old Diplomacy, but also of culture. There is, one gathers, nothing more to be said for art than Mr. Parham, in the National Gallery, says to Sir Bussy Woodcock. And the book ends with Sir Bussy (representative and defence-mechanism of Mr. Wells) declaring of a proposed newspaper propaganda to Mr. Parham: 'It would be up against everything you are.' 'History is bunk!' said Mr. Henry Ford. Mr. Wells, who is an authority, endorses.

Sir Bussy's is not the only scheme for using a civilized technique on behalf of a civilizing education. Dr. John B. Watson (who is vice-president of an advertising concern), writes: [1]

> We hear of no technique for learning how to behave emotionally or unemotionally. Anybody can teach you to play tennis, drive a motor-car, set type, to paint or to draw. We have schools and instructors for all this, but who has set up a school for teaching us to be afraid and not afraid, to fall in love and to fall out of love, to be jealous or not jealous, to be slow to anger and quick to forget, not to let the sun go down on our wrath, to forgive freely, not to give way to angry passions? And yet some of these modes of behaviour make up the essence of the Christian religion, as a matter of fact, they are part of every civilized code.

So Dr. Watson explains the technique that is to replace the unscientific traditional ways. As for standards of moral and other value, he is modest: he does not dictate:

> It is not the behaviourist's business to say what is good for society. Society must make up its mind what it wants

---

[1] *The Ways of Behaviourism*, p. 48.

its members to be and to do; then it is up to the behaviourist to find the methods and technique that will bring the child up in the way it should grow.[1]

He has misgivings, it is true:

> The behaviourist, then, has given society the rough pattern of a new weapon for controlling the individual. Will it use this weapon when perfected as a steam roller to flatten out all that is different in human personalities (which it can do, in spite of 'heredity,' producing thereby a race of conformists)? Or will it use this method wisely?[2]

But even if Dr. Watson were in charge it would go ill with culture:

> The new things in the universe come from the doers— the chemist, the physicist, the engineer, the biologist, the business man. With them doing leads to thinking, and thinking in turn leads to doing. With the poet, the day-dreamer, thinking leads not to doing but *merely to other words* either spoken or thought; the endless chain of words is never broken.[3]

> We have too many philosophic verbal speculators, rhetoricians, poets and dreamers now.[4]

Dr. Watson, of course, is an American and in England regarded as a crank. But there is reason to suppose that Behaviourism has already had a good deal of practical effect in America. And, in any case, Dr. Watson only exhibits in an extreme form traits commonly to be observed in highly intelligent and disinterested persons of scientific training who devote themselves to the future of humanity. Anyone who has met a Eugenist will recognize these traits. Major Leonard Darwin, President of the Eugenics Education Society, for instance, thinks that human excellence may, for practical Eugenic pur-

[1] *The Ways of Behaviourism*, pp. 60–1. [2] *Ibid.*, p. 63.
[3] *Ibid.*, p. 86. [4] *Ibid.*, p. 111.

poses, be measured by earning capacity.[1]   Then there is
Sir Richard Paget, author of the recent important book,
Human Speech.   In a little book called *Babel*, published
in the *To-day and To-morrow* series, Sir Richard argues,
cogently, that it is time English was deliberately and
scientifically improved and standardized as a language of
thought.   'Broadcasting, long-distance telephony, the
talking film, and the gramophone,' he says truly, 'will
make such standardization possible, and even comparatively easy to establish.'   Anything else a language may
be besides a 'method of symbolizing human thought' he
considers as so little important that he can say:

> If the keepers of our language maintain a die-hard
> attitude and succeed in preventing reasoned improvement,
> the result will, I suggest, be that language will be less and
> less used for intellectual and rational purposes, and rele-
> gated to an altogether inferior status as the symbolism of
> sentiment and small talk.

This is the only recognition Sir Richard gives to
English Literature.   He, too, proposes to use compulsion:
he would suppress Mr. James Joyce, or, rather, the future
die-hard of Mr. Joyce's kind:

> I can see no alternative but that there should, eventually,
> be a censorship of words, and that the printing or use in
> public of such improper words should be forbidden.

It is no laughing matter: Sir Richard Paget does in
some way represent enlightenment as against conservative
inertia.   On the one hand, the academic custodians of
tradition are what they are.   On the other, there is so
strong a case to be made out for some such reform as
Sir Richard Paget advocates.   No one aware of the
situation and concerned about the future of Shakespeare's
language can view quite happily the interest taken by
some of the most alert minds of our day in such a scheme

---

[1] *The Need for Eugenic Reform*, Major Leonard Darwin.

as 'Basic English.' [1] This instrument, embodying the extreme of analytical economy, is, of course, intended for a limited use. But what hope is there that the limits will be kept? If 'Basic English' proves as efficacious as it promises it will not remain a mere transition language for the Chinese. What an excellent instrument of education it would make, for instance, in the English-speaking countries! And, if hopes are fulfilled, the demand for literature in 'Basic English' will grow to vast dimensions as Asia learns how to use this means of access to the West. It seems incredible that the English language as used in the West should not be affected, especially in America, where it is so often written as if it were not native to the writer, and where the general use of it is so little subject to control by sentimental conservatism. Mass-production and standardization have not achieved their supreme triumph yet:

> Meanwhile the president of the Radio Corporation of America proclaims an era at hand when 'the oldest and the newest civilization will throb together at the same intellectual appeal, and to the same artistic emotions.' [2]

We cannot be indifferent in the face of such possibilities. For, as we noted above, when we used the metaphor of 'language' in defining culture we were using more than a metaphor. The most important part of this 'language' is actually a matter of the use of words. Without the living subtlety of the finest idiom (which is dependent upon use) the heritage dies.[3] It is a measure of the

[1] *Vide Basic English*, C. K. Ogden, and *Carl and Anna in Basic English* (Psyche Miniatures Series).

[2] *Middletown*, p. 268.

[3] 'From the beginning civilization has been dependent upon speech, for words are our chief link with the past and with one another and the channel of our spiritual inheritance. As the other vehicles of tradition, the family and the community, for example, are dissolved, we are forced more and more to reply upon language.'— *Practical Criticism*, pp. 320–1.

desperateness of the situation that intelligent people, when this is put to them, should be able to reply: 'Oh, but you can go on using *your* language: what does it matter what the rest of the world does?' So difficult can it be for really alert and unprejudiced minds to-day to understand what it is that is being discussed: things have gone so far already.

The prospects of culture, then, are very dark. There is the less room for hope in that a standardized civilization is rapidly enveloping the whole world. The glimpse of Russia that is permitted us does not afford the comfort that we are sometimes invited to find there. Anyone who has seen Eisenstein's film, *The General Line*, will appreciate the comment made by a writer in the *New Republic* (June 4th, 1930), comparing it with an American film:

> One fancies, thinking about these things, that America might well send *The Silent Enemy* to Russia and say, 'This is what living too long with too much machinery does to people. Think twice, before you commit yourselves irrevocably to the same course.'

But it is vain to resist the triumph of the machine. It is equally vain to console us with the promise of a 'mass culture' that shall be utterly new. It would, no doubt, be possible to argue that such a 'mass culture' might be better than the culture we are losing, but it would be futile: the 'utterly new' surrenders everything that can interest us.[1]

What hope, then, is there left to offer? The vague hope that recovery *must* come, somehow, in spite of all?

---

[1] ' . . . indeed, this gentleman, taking the bull by the horns, proposes that we should for the future call industrialism culture, and then of course there can be no longer any misapprehension of their true character; and besides the pleasure of being wealthy and comfortable, they will have authentic recognition as vessels of sweetness and light.'—*Culture and Anarchy.*

Mr. I. A. Richards seems to authorize hope: he speaks of 'reasons for thinking that this century is in a cultural trough rather than upon a crest'; and says that 'the situation is likely to get worse before it is better.' [1] 'Once the basic level has been reached,' he suggests, 'a slow climb back may be possible. That at least is a hope that may be reasonably entertained.' [2] But it is a hope that looks very desperate in face of the downward acceleration described above, and it does not seem to point to any factor that might be counted upon to reverse the process.

Are we then to listen to Spengler's [3] (and Mr. Henry Ford's [4]) admonition to cease bothering about the inevitable future? That is impossible. Ridiculous, priggish and presumptuous as it may be, if we care at all about the issues we cannot help believing that, for the immediate future, at any rate, we have some responsibility. We cannot help clinging to some such hope as Mr. Richards offers; to the belief (unwarranted, possibly) that what we value most matters too much to the race to be finally

---

[1] *Practical Criticism*, p. 320.

[2] *Ibid.*, p. 249.

[3] 'Up to now everyone has been at liberty to hope what he pleased about the future. Where there are no facts, sentiment rules. But henceforward it will be every man's business to inform himself of what *can* happen and therefore of what with the unalterable necessity of destiny and irrespective of personal ideals, hopes or desires, *will* happen.'—*The Decline of the West*, Vol. I, p. 39.

[4] 'But what of the future? Shall we not have over-production? Shall we not some day reach a point where the machine becomes all powerful, and the man of no consequence?

'No man can say anything of the future. We need not bother about it. The future has always cared for itself in spite of our well-meant efforts to hamper it. If to-day we do the task we can best do, then we are doing all that we can do.

'Perhaps we may over-produce, but that is impossible until the whole world has all its desires. And if that should happen, then surely we ought to be content.'—Henry Ford, *To-day and To-morrow*, pp. 272–3.

abandoned, and that the machine will yet be made a tool.

It is for us to be as aware as possible of what is happening, and, if we can, to 'keep open our communications with the future.'